Baedeker's
VENICE

Imprint

Cover picture:
Torre dell'Orologio: clock tower with bronze Moors and the Lion of St. Mark

46 colour photographs
8 plans, 1 large city map

Conception: Redaktionsbüro Harenberg Schwerte

Text: Ulrich Ritter

Editorial work and additional material:
Baedeker-Redaktion

General direction:
Dr. Peter Baumgarten, Baedeker, Stuttgart

Editorial work and additional text, English language edition:
Alec Court

English translation: Babel Translations Norwich

Cartography:
Ingenieurbüro für Kartographie Huber & Oberländer, Munich
Georg Schiffner, Lahr (city map)

Source of illustrations:
dpa (9), Historia-Photo (9), Huber (1), Italian State Tourist Office (1), Provincial Tourist Office (1), Rogge (9), Storto (1), Uthoff (15)

Following the tradition established by Karl Baedeker in 1844, sights of particular interest and hotels of outstanding quality are distinguished by either one or two asterisks.

To make it easier to locate the various sights listed in the "A to Z" section of the Guide, their coordinates on the large map of central Venice are shown in red at the head of each entry.

Only a selection of hotels, restaurants and shops can be given: no reflection is implied, therefore, on establishments not included.

In a time of rapid change it is difficult to ensure that all the information given is entirely accurate and up to date, and the possibility of error can never be entirely eliminated. Although the publishers can accept no responsibility for inaccuracies and omissions they are always grateful for corrections and suggestions for improvement.

Contents

Preface

This Pocket Guide to Venice is one of the new generation of Baedeker city guides.

Baedeker pocket guides, illustrated throughout in colour, are designed to meet the needs of the modern traveller. They are quick and easy to consult, with the principal sights described in alphabetical order and practical details about opening times, how to get there, etc., shown in the margin.

Each guide is divided into three parts. The first part gives a general account of the city, its history, population, culture and so on; in the second part the principal sights are described; and the third part contains a variety of practical information designed to help visitors to find their way about and make the most of their stay.

The new guides are abundantly illustrated and contain numbers of newly drawn plans. At the back of the book is a large city map, and each entry in the main part of the guide gives the coordinates of the square on the map in which the particular feature can be located. Users of this guide, therefore will have no difficulty in finding what they want to see.

Facts and Figures

General

Venice, in Italian Venezia, is the capital of the Veneto region, one of the 20 "regions" of the Republic of Italy. Officially entitled "Venezia Città", the city is situated in the north-eastern part of Italy on longitude 12° 2' E and latitude 41° 25' N.

Situation

The present commune of Greater Venice includes Marghera and Mestre on the mainland, the islands of Torcello, Burano and Murano, the part of the city on the Lido and Venice proper, i.e. the historical island city in the middle of the lagoon. The many islands upon which Venice itself is built cover an area of 7·06 sq. km (2·7 sq. miles). It is 4,260 m (about 3 miles) long and from 2,790 m (about 2 miles) wide at its broadest point to 1,330 m (about 1 mile) at its narrowest. The circumference of the city, including the islands of San Giorgio and Giudecca, amounts to 13·7 km (about 9 miles). Of the 370,000 living in Greater Venice, about 108,000 live in Venice proper.

Area and population

The Venetians speak a marked Italian dialect of their own. Not only is their pronunciation more softened than any other dialect, they also change actual words of Italian: brothers, for example, is "frari" instead of "frati", house is "ca'" instead of "casa", angel "anzelo" instead of "angelo", and fish "pesse" istead of "pesce".
The written Venetian dialect is also encountered throughout Venice in the nameplates for canals, streets, buildings, etc.

Venetian dialect

For centuries the city in the lagoon has been divided into six districts or "sestieri": these are San Marco, Castello, Cannaregio, Santa Croce, San Polo and Dorsoduro (which includes Giudecca and San Giorgio). Houses are numbered consecutively up to 5,000 and above for each sestieri, which makes for a system that is almost incomprehensible for anyone who is not a Venetian.

Districts

Venice elected its first Doge as early as 697 and, with its constitutional reforms in the 11th and 12th c., created an aristocratic oligarchy and the Western World's first Republic, where the Great Council and the Senate limited the previously absolute power of the Doge. This aristocratic republic succeeded in maintaining its independence until it fell to Napoleon in 1797 and made it possible for Venice to achieve the status of a World Power and one of the world's centres of commerce.
Nowadays Greater Venice, like every Italian city, is governed by a Sindaco (Mayor) and Giunta Municipale (Municipal Council). Local government elections are held every five years.

Administration

Venice – city of the lagoon

Venice lies in the Laguna Veneta, a salt-water lagoon 40 km (25 miles) long and up to 15 km (9¼ miles) wide. This lagoon was formed in prehistoric times by silt deposits that built up an

Laguna Veneta

almost unbroken line of spits (the lidi, sing. Lido) about 20 km (12½ miles) out to sea from the flat Adriatic coastline. A breach in the spit was called a "porto" (pl. "porti").

Island city

Further deposits of mud formed islands within the lagoon and the original settlements on these islands gradually grew together to form Venice.

The city remained cut off as an island until 1846 when the causeway was built to the mainland to carry the railway line.

City on piles

Venice consists of 118 flat islets, packed close together, and originally, because of their soft mud covering, considered unsuitable for buildings. The settlers then discovered that there was a solid layer of heavy clay beneath the mud and that buildings could be erected on piles driven down into this substratum. A horizontal layer of piling was then placed on top of the vertical piles, thus providing the foundations for almost all of Venice's 20,000 or so buildings.

Venice in Peril

Venice is in peril because Venice is slowly sinking. The sinking is caused by two factors: the rising of the Adriatic (due to melting of Polar ice-caps) and the pumping of water from the subsoil. Since the construction of aqueducts supplying alternative water-supply to the industrial complex of Marghera, the sinking has been considerably slowed down.

International organisations are trying to save the city. Almost every European country, as well as the USA and Australia, has taken on the sponsorship of particularly important buildings. Since the disastrous flooding in 1966 there have been innumerable conferences to look at ways of saving the city from "drowning" or decay through industrial pollution. In 1985 it was finally decided to embark on a ten-year project: at three entrances to the lagoon dykes are to be built and barriers consisting of gigantic tank-like cylinders constructed which can be raised or lowered according to the water level. It remains to be seen whether these measures will protect Venice from exceptionally high tides without endangering the essential ebb and flow of water in the canals and lagoons which has occured twice daily for hundreds of years with high and low tides.

Population and Religion

Population

The Venetians are the descendants of an Illyrian tribe, the Veneti, who, until they were conquered by Rome in the 3rd c. B.C., settled the Adriatic Plain N of the River Po. Nowadays about 108,000 people still live in historic Venice, while a further 260,000 or so live in the neighbouring industrial districts of Mestre and Marghera whose refineries and dockyards attract a workforce from the whole of Italy.

Only about 2,000 people still commute daily from historic Venice to work in the industrial zones, as compared with 10 times that number who commute from the mainland every day to work in the island city.

Religion

The Venetians are 99% Roman Catholic. Their Cardinal Archbishop bears the title of Patriarch. Pope John XXIII was Patriarch of Venice before his election to the Papacy.

People in Venice

Transport

The new economy of Venice is centred on the port of Marghera. Dating primarily from after the First World War, this has become, with its annual turnover of 24 million tons of goods, 24 km (15 miles) of quayside and enormous container port, Italy's second largest industrial port.

As an oil terminal, however, Marghera can hardly compete with Trieste, which can also accommodate supertankers. Although the channel through the lagoon has been dredged, there are no

Port

11

discharge facilities for oil-tankers of a tonnage greater than 90,000 because of the relatively shallow waters in this part of the Mediterranean.

Passenger shipping

The port for passenger ships is in the Canale di San Marco, diagonally opposite the Doge's Palace. There are connections with all the main Adriatic ports as well as with Rhodes and Piraeus in Greece; Venice is also popular as the point of embarkation for cruises which usually leave from Zattere and the Riva degli Schiavoni.

Airport

The airport for Venice, Marco Polo International Airport (Aeroporto Internazionale), is 13 km (8 miles) NE of Venice, near Tessera.

Railway

Since 1846 a railway bridge has linked the "Santa Lucia" railway terminal on the island of Venice with the mainland and the rest of the international rail network; Venice is served by direct express trains from virtually all the main European destinations.

Exit roads

Since 1933 Venice has also been joined to the mainland by a roadbridge linking it with the Italian road system and, via the Milan–Trieste motorway, also with the European motorway network.
Cars cannot be taken beyond the Tronchetto car park or the multi-storey car park at the Piazzale Roma at the end of the roadbridge. Beyond that point all movement in the city is either by boat or on foot.

Boats

Since the 118 islands that go to make up Venice are crammed very close together and are built on up to the very edges, while the waterways between the individual islands have been kept open, Venice has a network of 177 canals, most of them narrow, which act as the streets of the city. Nowadays the main means of transport is by the various types of motor boat, but the traditional barges and gondolas, operated by only one person, are still very much in evidence as are the troghetti (gondola ferries) which are craft rowed by more than one person.
Craft that operate a regular passenger service can be found on the Canal Grande and its continuation to the eastern tip of the city, as well as from the Riva degli Schiavoni and from Zattere to San Giorgio and Giudecca. There is also a circle line with craft travelling round the periphery of the city.
For journeys over a longer distance there are only two embarkation points, the Riva degli Schiavoni (for the Lido, Chioggia, Punta Sabbioni) and Fondamente Nuove (for Murano, Burano and Torcello). All other journeys have to be made on foot, unless you wish to hire a gondola or motor boat to serve as a taxi.

Gondolas

The gondolas are the oldest type of boat in Venice (first mentioned in 697) and have since that time served primarily to carry passengers. Their number has shrunk from 10,000 in the 16th c. to only 500 today. In 1562 it was decreed that in future all gondolas must be painted black since the noble houses were overloading their craft with ornamentation. Every gondola is 10·15 m (33¼ ft) long and 1·40 m (4½ ft) wide and has a toothed projection forward, called the "ferro", to balance the weight of the gondolier who stands in the stern. Eight different types of wood are used in a gondola, which weighs 700 kg (1,543 lb).

Gondolas – for centuries Venice's prime means of transport

The embodiment of the glory of Venice is the Canal Grande, the Grand Canal, which winds like an inverted "S" through the city, thus dividing it into two halves. It is one of the tributaries of the River Brenta which flows through the lagoon at this point out into the sea. The knolls on the banks of this tributary projecting above the waters of the lagoon formed the island on which Venice stands, hence the time-honoured name of "Rivus Altus" (High Bank) or, in its present form, Rialto.

Canal Grande

With its length of 3·8 km (2·4 miles) and its width of from 40 to 70 m (130 to 230 ft), the Canal Grande is the largest of Venice's canals and with its magnificent palaces on either side has become one of the most famous "high streets" in the world.

Besides its canals Venice also has 3,000 streets. Apart from the general term "calle" these are also called "Fondamenta" or "Riva" (formerly embankment), 'Salizzada" (main street), "Rugo" or "Rugetta" (alley), "Ramo" (cul de sac), "Lista" (formerly the site of the foreign embassies) and, finally, "Rio terrà" (filled-in canal). There is only one "Piazza", namely the Square of St Mark, and the smaller adjoining squares are called "Piazetta" (in front of the Doges' Palace, see Palazzo Ducale, and the Piazetta dei Leoncini, near the Basilica of San Marco, see entry). All Venice's other squares are called "Campo" or, if they are very small, "Campiello".

Streets, squares, bridges

The streets and alleys cross the canals by means of more than 400 bridges, three of them over the Canal Grande: the wooden Ponte dell'Accademia, the famous Ponte di Rialto (see entries) and the modern Ponte Scalzi near the station.

Culture

Its famous buildings, art treasures and many academic establishments make Venice one of Italy's great centres of culture. It has a university, founded in 1868 for industry and commerce, colleges for architecture, music and foreign languages, an Academy of Sciences, an Art Academy, a nautical and oceanographic institute as well as other higher education establishments and technical colleges.

The Library of San Marco (1·2 million volumes) and the National Archive make their impact felt far beyond the confines of the city. As for museums, special mention should be made of the Museo Civico Correr, the Museo del Settecento Veneziano, the Archaeological Museum, the Museo d'Arte Moderna, the Galleria dell'Accademia, the Querini-Stampalia Picture Gallery, the Galleria Franchetti (see Ca' d'Oro), the Galleria Peggy Guggenheim (see Ca' Venier), the Museo Storico Navale and the Museo dell'Arte Vetraria (see Murano, glass museum).

In the 15th to 17th c. Venice became a renowned centre of art. The Venetian School of Painting began early in the 15th c. on Murano with Antonio and Bartolomeo Vivarini and went on to produce such famous artists as Titian, Tintoretto and Veronese (see Prominent Figures in Venetian History). The fame of Venetian painting underwent a resurgence in the Rococo period with Tiepolo, Canaletto and Guardi (see Prominent Figures in Venetian History).

In the field of music Venice played a prominent part with such innovators as Vivaldi and Monteverdi and in literature with Goldoni, a dramatist with a European reputation (see Prominent Figures in Venetian History).

Since the 19th c., when Venice capitulated to Napoleon, the city has failed to produce its own native-born artists but it has been the temporary home, particularly in the Romantic Period, of many internationally famed poets (Lord Byron, D'Annunzio) as well as theatrical personalities including Eleanora Duse.

Now Venice is again seeking to become a cultural centre. It hosts the "Biennale d'Arte (modern art exhibition) every two years and has an annual film festival, an international festival of contemporary music and opera seasons in La Fenice, as well as prestige performances in its theatres and a host of other different productions staged in its two open-air theatres.

Commerce and Industry

After centuries of economic decline today's Venice is again developing into a centre for commerce and industry, particularly in its suburbs of Mestre and Marghera which have a population of about 160,000 and where besides plant for processing cotton and agricultural products there are enormous refineries and dockyards as well as a viable metal-processing industry. Since the 1020s, when it was founded, this zone has grown to be a hive of industry and, as was intended, has come to provide the jobs needed by the people of Venice.

The island of Murano is the centre of the glass industry. The famous Murano glass is exported throughout the world, as well as proving a great tourist attraction. There are 300 glassworks, employing about 4,000 glassmakers.

For generations the people of the island of Burano have been making embroidered lace and throughout Venice there are many craftsmen engaged in turning out jewellery, textiles, etc. With its 200 hotels, the main industry of historic Venice (Venezia Città) is tourism and over half the working population is employed in the tourist trade. Venice is also the headquarters of banks and insurance companies, as well as an administrative centre.

Government of the Venetian City State under the Doges

Venice's situation between East and West and the political risks this engendered made it imperative to have a Constitution embodying checks and balances on political control. Venice was still a Republic which was represented by the Doge, underpinned by the aristocracy and ruled by two forces – the mutual interests of the patrician families and their fundamental and mutual mistrust of one another, of the Doge and of the people. The sole aim of the constitution was to neutralise any individual build-up of power and to ensure the two forces were evenly balanced.

Constitution

The people and the Church were soon eliminated from the political process; the power of the Doges was increasingly curbed. After 1229 the Doge of Venice had to swear to a "Promissio", to sign an agreement in which the electors stipulated the terms for the future government.

The Great Council, the Consiglio Maggior, was the real political power. Its members were the "Nobili", the aristocracy, whose interests, identical with the interests of the State, lay in trade, which must be pushed, promoted and protected.

It was not until late in the 16th and 17th c. when, with the discovery of new routes, trade took a different direction and Venice slowly declined in importance, that the interests of the nobility and the State were no longer identical.

If trade went well, then all was well with the city and with it the people and the polity. Individually the diverse interests which made up the State would have been incapable of embarking on the more risky ventures or of carrying out the more ambitious projects; collectively they had the strength, the power and the tenacity.

The Head of State for the Republic of Venice was the Doge, whose residence was in his palace (see A to Z, Palazzo Ducale). In A.D. 697 the first Doge, Pauluccio Anafesto, assumed office (Latin "Dux"=Italian Doge, cf. English Duke); in 1797 the last Doge, Manin, handed back the Doge's cap with the words "It will not be needed any more." Over those 1,100 years 120 Doges represented the Republic of Venice. Their badge of office, the Doge's cap, was based on the Phrygian fisherman's hat, rising to a point on a stiffened base, and set with gold and jewels to the value of 194,000 ducats.

Office of the Doge

Originally "primus inter pares" (first among equals), the Doge was elected and endorsed by the populace: "This is your Doge if he pleases you." His power was virtually boundless: he negotiated in his own right with Emperors and Popes, decided on war or peace, personally sought out his officials, his officers, his successor, often his co-Regents. His councillors ("Prega-di") had an advisory function only. He exercised jurisdiction and possessed the right of pardon.

When in 976 Doge Pietro Candiano IV (959–976) attempted to make the office of Doge hereditary and thus to alter the constitution to rule by a family there was a revolt. The Doge's Palace and the Basilica went up in flames and the Doge and his young son perished in San Marco.

This event prompted ever-more rigorous curbs on the power of the Doge: the law that the Doge could no longer appoint his co-Regents was followed by the law that the Doge could no longer appoint his successor (mid 11th c.). The Small Council (Consiglio Minore) was formed to watch over the Head of State. Finally the populace lost its voice in the election of the Doge – now it was "This is your Doge" (mid 12th c.) – and was replaced by the Great Council (Consiglio Maggiore).

Election of the Doge

As with the Pope, election took the form of a conclave. The balloting procedure was extremely complicated. Thirty members of the Great Council would be balloted for, and then the ballot would be for 9 of them. They nominated 40 provisional electors who in turn elected 12 by lot who then elected 25. These were reduced to 9 who then each nominated 5. These 45 were reduced by casting lots to 11; it needed 9 of the 11 votes to choose the final 41 who would elect the Doge.

The future Doge must amass at least 25 of these votes. He was elected for life. This system of election offered every noble the chance to take part without allowing any group or family to exercise undue influence and thus impair the basic principles of the Constitution.

Functions of the Doge

The office of the Doge, from the 13th c. onwards, was, in terms of political duties, more or less the equivalent of a modern State President: he represented the State at home and abroad, had a seat on every body in the Government (but only one vote), presided over the Great Council, had to bring about decisions and to control the officers of the State.

The list of duties that he could not undertake was, however, entirely geared to the specific interests of the Republic and its Constitution, which, as such, was unique in the world. A catalogue of those duties that were not open to him was drawn up in 1600: the Doge was not allowed to appoint his own men nor could he hold any external office (this affected Doge Enrico Dandolo, conqueror of Byzantium, who was not allowed to accept the Crown of Austria). No member of the Doge's family was allowed to take part in a business venture; sons and daughters could not marry outside the Republic without the permission of the Great Council. The Doge must swear in the Promissio (see Constitution) not to undertake any coup, not to seek to restore the former powers of the office, not to open any letters from outside Powers in the absence of the Councils, not to write any, not to receive envoys, not to accept presents (other than flowers, herbs or rosewater). His Councillors (Pregadi) were appointed by the Great Council. He was no longer allowed to erect or improve public buildings, to have any possessions other than those connected with his office of Doge.

Finally in the 16th and 17th c. came still further restrictions: even in his private apartments he was forbidden to receive foreign envoys or generals. His sons were not permitted to go out of the State; his Consort was no longer to be crowned and no longer had an official retinue. Similarly he and his family were forbidden to maintain relations with outside sovereigns. Although in the early years of the office the Doge still was at the head of the army, after the 14th c. the duty was hardly exercised. If he should appear on the battlefield it was to embolden his people, not to lead them. There was one exception: in 1684 Doge Francesco Morosini succeeded in winning back the Peloponnese for 30 years. In the course of the fighting a Venetian shell blew up the Parthenon on the Acropolis in Athens.

After 1172 the Great Council, which drew together the great noble families of the Republic, became the supreme legislative body of the State and watchdog over the Doge. In the early 13th c. the Great Council had 35 members. When this number had risen steeply the Council, in 1297, enacted a "Serrata" decreeing that from thenceforward no one whose family was not recorded in the "Libro d'Oro", the register of the aristocracy of the Republic, could become a member of the Council (when the Republic ended there were 1,218 names in this Golden Book).

Great Council

The Great Council was only directly consulted on absolutely basic matters and confined itself otherwise to the acceptance of statements of accounts but its members did determine the membership of the different bodies charged with executing the affairs of State, and it elected the Doge from its own ranks. Each noble held an office in the State organisation, usually as an unpaid servant of the State. He was not allowed either to refuse any duty he was called upon to discharge or decline any command. Anyone who failed when in office, whether or not it was his own fault, was subject to the harshest penalties.

Their compliance with the strict laws created by the members of the Great Council in the interests of the State was as unquestioning and unconditional as the obedience they required of the other members of the polity.

The middle-class families were recorded in the Silver Book. Although they took no part in the decision-making process, they were responsible for overseeing and running the administration of the State and putting the Government decrees into effect. The families recorded in the Gold and Silver Books did not amount to as much as 15% of Venice's population but they owned almost 90% of its capital assets.

Silver Book

After 976 the Senate or "Small Council" gradually came to be the supervisory body for the Doges. It was not until 1229 that it became an official authority, with narrowly defined tasks and the title of "Consiglio dei Pregadi" (its members were requested, i.e. "pregadi" or prayed, to attend the sessions by a written invitation). The Senate consisted of 60 members elected from the Great Council, the Doge and the "Zonta", which was made up of 6 patricians from the Great Council, 5 representatives of the provinces on the mainland and 5 representatives of the religious Orders. Other members of the circle were the closest of the Doge's advisers, the delegates from the Judiciary, the Council of Ten, the "Avvogadori" (constitutional judges), the "Cattaveri" (tax assessors) and the "Provveditori" (overseers).

Senate (Small Council)

Government under the Doges

The Senate was in effect the governing Parliament - answerable to the Great Council but entitled to take major decisions: it decided on peace or war, what decrees should be submitted to the Great Council and appointed all important State officials, office-holders, bishops and prelates. It also set up and supervised all the committees charged with aligning the administration to political and social developments.

Collegio

The Collegio was the Cabinet of the Republic of St Mark. It was composed of the Doge and his six Councillors, the three Magistrates who presided over the Courts of Justice and the chairmen of the three groups in the Zonta. The Collegio prepared all the Bills to be submitted to the Senate, decided on what should be kept from the Senate on grounds of secrecy, received and heard foreign envoys and was responsible for the delicate negotiations with the Church of Rome. In addition it was the supreme court of appeal for the Judiciary. Also the Collegio acted on behalf of the Republic in dealing with representatives of Foreign Powers. Its members were elected from the Great Council and the Senate.

Council of Ten

The Council of Ten, the most sinister and most feared body in the Venetian Government, was meant to act as a liaison between the legislature, i.e. the Great Council and the Senate, and the executive, i.e. the Doge, and the Administration – such as the judiciary. It was called into being when in 1310 Baiamonte Tiepolo made a vain attempt to break the rule of the nobility, but did not emerge in its final form until the Decree of the Great Council in 1455.

The Senate decided every year on the 10 members of this Council. The Doge and his six councillors also sat in on the Council of Ten, together with a constitutional lawyer (Avvocador) whose job it was to ensure that the decisions of the Council of Ten accorded with the laws and the constitution. The names of the members of the Council of Ten were kept secret.

The multifarious tasks and duties of the Council of Ten can be summed up as guarding State security. They were mainly concerned with dealing with matters of planned, attempted or accomplished high treason, espionage, sabotage, conspiracy, etc. The Council was also responsible for keeping watch on the morals of the city, and preventing and punishing suspected duels (which were strictly forbidden), violent acts and anything that amounted to a disturbance of the peace. And finally the Council was charged with pursuing acts endangering trade and assuming the responsibility for getting the greatest possible yields from the State enterprises such as the glass industry or mining and forestry on the mainland.

The Council of Ten was the absolute organ of public safety with virtually unlimited powers. It was a watchdog over the most intimate life of the citizen and against its verdict there was no appeal, even in the event of summary judgements meted out without preamble. Any Venetian could be summoned before the Council, even the Doge, and Marin Falier, the Doge executed in 1355 for alleged high treason, was only one among many. It was also up to the Council of Ten, after the death of a Doge, to judge how he had fulfilled his office and those who were left behind had to bear the brunt of the praise, censure or even damages arising from any blunders.

For these extremely onerous official duties the Council of Ten had three invaluable aids at its disposal:

(1) an efficient and unobtrusive secret police, that could do its bidding in any corner of the world;

(2) the "lions' mouths", the letterboxes for secret denunciations. Any Venetian who noticed anything suspicious could turn this into a denunciation by writing it down and posting his communication in a "lion's mouth". He had to sign it, together with two witnesses (a necessary measure to prevent malicious or defamatory denunciations), but the person denounced would never know who it was had denounced him;

(3) the merchant traders. The merchants of Venice, travelling on every sea and in almost every part of the civilised world, were always on the spot for gathering the very best information about trade and politics – in the markets and the bazaars, and in the Courts of the powerful. And every returning Venetian merchant not only brought back with him a ship full of wares but also proved a mine of information for the secret service.

For centuries the Government of the Venetian Republic was the best-informed Government in the world – further grounds for the city's rise to power.

The Council of Ten could count upon these three aids and usually knew exactly what it was about! As a rule everything happened very swiftly; suddenly the secret police would appear, arrest the suspect and whisk him away to appear before the Council. The accusation would be read out and if it could not be conclusively refuted the accused would immediately be found guilty. If the miserable wretch still did not confess, this would be followed by the torture – and then the sentence which could be a flogging, the loss of a hand, gouging out the eyes, etc. but in about half the cases the sentence was death. The famous executions between the Colonne di Marco e Teodoro (see entry) on the Molo were relatively rare. More often than not the condemned were discreetly throttled in their cells or taken out to sea at night and drowned in the lagoon between San Giorgio and the Lido.

Anyone condemned "in absentia" was also as good as dead, even if he thought himself safely abroad. The Council of Ten had its secret police, and the police had their "Venetian dagger", a razor-sharp blade of glass, sheathed in metal, as broad as a man's thumb, which, when plunged into the victim's body up to the hilt, would immediately snap off at the haft. The victim's skin would straightaway close up over the wound, leaving what appeared to be only a slight graze at the point of entry. It was some considerable time before the rest of the world caught up with this particular Venetian secret weapon.

The fact that the Council of Ten also supervised the preparations for important State ceremonies and receptions and even had a hand, in the background, in their organisation, shows how wide was the range of their duties.

The "Chiefs" jointly conducted examinations and brought them to the Council of Ten for their decision. They consisted of two members of the Ten and one of the Doge's Councillors. If they felt a communication was too dangerous it was not shown to the Council of Ten or the Doge but lodged in the form of a sealed document.

Three Chief Magistrates (Inquisitori)

Although termed simply "advocates" these lawyers in fact acted as judges of the Constitution and public prosecutors. It

Three Avvogadori

was their job to ensure that decisions in the Great Council, the Senate and the Council of Ten accorded with the laws and if necessary they could exercise their veto. They also watched over the observance of treaties, the collection of fines and the correctness of commercial and private legal procedures.

The institution of the "Avvogadori", which had existed since the 12th c., was, therefore, a precursor of the independent administration of justice that exists today in all democratic States. In this sense it should be considered in conjunction with the "Quarantia".

Quarantia

This institution, consisting of 40 (i.e. "quaranta") members, had existed since 1179. Originally merely a court of appeal of no more than 40 patricians, it rapidly developed into the actual judicial body of the Republic. In the 14th c. its workload was so great that the "Quarantia" had to be split up and become twofold. It became the Quarantia Civil, the court dealing with civil cases, and Quarantia Criminal, responsible for non-political criminal cases such as murder, robbery, etc. Two hundred years later the civil complaints, such as defamation, fraud, etc. had become so numerous that the Quarantia Civil had to be further subdivided into the Quarantia Civil Vecchia and the Quarantia Civil Nuova.

Provveditori, Cattaveri, Censori

All these State organs gradually created a network of honorary or paid officials and institutions that painstakingly performed the duties they were charged with.

Chief among these were the Provveditori, the overseers, nobles who superintended and directed indispensable organisations and projects. Hence the "Provveditori de Mar", a body responsible for fitting out the war fleet, recruiting seamen and rowers, etc., or Provveditori who looked after the welfare institutions or were concerned with the churches, monasteries and religious associations.

Less obtrusive but much less pleasant were the Cattaveri, the tax assessors. Every Venetian, regardless of rank and person, had to allow them to inspect absolutely everything he possessed and then let the assessor dictate to him how much – and always it was a considerable sum – he had to pay the State in taxes. And woe betide anyone making a false declaration: they would soon find themselves arraigned in front of the Council of Ten.

Last but by no means least there were the "Censori". Drawn from the Great Council, their sole task was to prevent cheating in the elections for the various bodies and offices. It is said – and this speaks for the honour of the Republic of St Mark – that throughout all those centuries their services were hardly ever called upon.

Prominent Figures in Venetian History

Canaletto was one of the last of the great Venetian artists. Born in Venice, he started painting in the theatre then studied in Rome and turned to nature studies. His first great success in Venice was with "vedute" (views) then after a second stay in Rome in 1742 he started painting imaginary landscapes before finally taking up the genre which he made all his own of finely detailed townscapes alive with carnivals, festivals and processions.

Canaletto spent two periods in England (1746–50 and 1751–53) and it is there that most of his works can be found. In Venice a "capriccio" by Canaletto is to be seen in the Accademia di Belle Arti.

Canaletto
(Giovanni Antonio Canal)
(18.10.1697–20.4.1768)

His fame as a lover and his elegant philandering have made Giacomo Casanova a legendary son of Venice. His invented title of "Chevalier de Seingalt" point to his being by nature an adventurer. He made a spectacular escape from the Venetian State Prison by a peculiarly hazardous route. On his travels throughout Europe (in various posts) he broke many a maidenly heart. Constantly embroiled in disputes and frequently on the run, Casanova finally found a post in 1785 as Librarian to Count Waldstein in Bohemia where he wrote his "Memoirs" (in French), an important record of the society of his day. He also penned a Utopian novel and other historical, mathematical and scientific works.

Giacomo Casanova
(2.4.1725–4.6.1798)

Dandolo, scion of an old-established noble Venetian family, was 82 before he was elected Doge. Despite his age he never shrank from any military confrontation that might secure and advance Venetian influence in the Eastern Mediterranean and thus he drove the Pisans out of Istria. As a greybeard of 94 and totally blind, with the lords of the Fourth Crusade, he helped conquer the Byzantine Empire of the Eastern Church. On the fall of Constantinople and Dalmatia he secured for Venice a great share of the treasures captured as booty, built staging-posts on the route to Constantinople and finally made Venice into a World Power. He died in 1205 in Constantinople.

Enrico Dandolo
(c. 1110–14.6.1205)

Francesco Foscari, elected Doge in 1423, continued the Venetian policy of expansion; after 1426 he conducted the four Milanese wars with the other Northern Italian city states and secured for the city its greatest territorial expansion – from Brescia to Ravenna. In 1454 the Peace of Lodi ended the centuries of fighting for sovereignty in Northern Italy. During this time, however, Foscari neglected policy in the East so in 1454 he finally had to sign a treaty with the Sultan abandoning Venice's supremacy in the Eastern Mediterranean.

In 1407 Foscari was deposed, thanks to the opposition of the Lorendano family, and his son Jacopo was banished. His fate and that of his oft-banished son inspired poets (Lord Byron) and composers (Verdi).

Francesco Foscari
(c. 1373–1.11.1457)

Prominent Figures in Venetian History

Giacomo Casanova

Carlo Goldoni

Claudio Monteverdi

Carlo Goldoni
(25.2.1707–6.2.1793)

The only great poetic writer in the history of that city of commerce, Venice, Goldoni introduced realism into Italian comedy, superseding the commedia dell'arte with comedies of manners that had much in common with Molière. He wrote as many as 136 comedies, including "The Servant of Two Masters" and "La Locandiera".

After studying law and philosophy Goldoni worked from 1744 to 1748 as a lawyer in Pisa, but his youthful involvement with the theatre led him on his return to Venice to begin writing plays from 1748 to 1753 for the Teatro di Sant'Angelo and then, until 1762, for the Teatro di San Luca.

In 1762 the competition from rival playwrights caused Goldoni to leave for Paris where he was the Director of the Italian Theatre until 1764 and also mounted productions of his own plays. Impoverished by the Revolution, he died in 1793.

Claudio Monteverdi
(15.5.1567–29.11.1643)

The impact of Claudio Monteverdi on music continued into the 18th c.

Born in Cremona, Monteverdi was originally a scholar of composition in his home town (until 1590) and then a musician and Choirmaster at the Court of Mantura (until 1612). From 1613 until his death he worked as the Choirmaster of San Marco in Venice.

Moving away from the rigid musical forms of the 16th c. Monteverdi developed greater freedom in styles of music but what made him, as the creator of "Orfeo", "Ulisse" and "Poppea", the first great opera-composer, whose influence was to be felt by such contrasting composers as Gluck and Richard Wagner, was his innovatory power of conceiving the drama as a whole in terms of music.

Marco Polo
(1254–8.1.1324)

Marco Polo, whose travels changed the concept of the world of his time and focused the attention of Europeans on the distant East, was 17 when in 1271 his father and uncle took him with them from Venice on their journey to trade with China. After taking over three years crossing the continent of Asia they arrived at the Court of Kublai Khan, the Mongol Emperor. Marco Polo spent the next 17 years holding high office and travelling in the service of the Khan who finally in 1292 gave his permission for them to return to Europe. Marco Polo's account of his travels was dictated to his fellow captive Rusticiano

Marco Polo

Tintoretto

Antonio Vivaldi

during his sojourn in a Genoese gaol (1298–99). After his release he returned to Venice where he died in 1324.

The Florentine Sansovino left his mark as no other architect could on the townscape of Venice when after 1527 he was appointed First Architect and Engineer of the Republic. He had a hand in or was responsible for the building of no less than 15 of the city's churches and public buildings including the Library of San Marco, the Mint (now the Biblioteca Marciana), the Logetta di San Marco, the Church of San Francesco della Vigna, the Palazzo Correr and the statues of Mars and Neptune in the courtyard of the Doge's Palace.
He died in the city in 1570 at the age of 84.

Sansovino
(Jacopo Tatti)
(2.7.1486–27.11.1570)

Tintoretto not only holds a place in the annals of Venetian art as an indefatigable, inspired artist but also owes his place in history to being an artist with a businesslike approach. The son of a silk-dyer – "tintore" – and hence his name.
Born in Venice, he left the city only once in his lifetime (he is known to have journeyed to Mantua in 1580) but was, nevertheless, influenced by the major artists of his time (e.g. Michelangelo) and the influence of Titian is apparent in the contrasting effects of light and shade in his paintings. The themes of his work tended to be taken from the Old and New Testaments.
His work in Venice can be found in the Galleria dell'Accademia ("The Miracle of St Mark", "Cain and Abel"), in the Church of San Giorgio Maggiore ("The Last Supper"), in San Marcuola ("The Last Supper"), in the Church of Santa Maria della Salute ("The Wedding at Cana"), in the Church of Santa Maria Mater Domini ("The Finding of the True Cross by St Helena"), in the Church of San Rocco ("The Healing of the Stricken") and, above all, in the Scuola di San Rocco ("Christ before Pilate", "Christ Carrying the Cross", "Moses Striking Water from the Rock", "The Feeding of the Five Thousand").

Tintoretto
(Jacopo Robusti)
(29.9.1518–31.5.1594)

In the middle of the 16th c. Titian, descendant of a family of artists, was the most sought-after painter in all Europe. He is thought to have come to Venice in 1508, where he was taught by Bellini and Giorgione and worked with them on their

Titian
(Tiziano Vecellio)
(c. 1477–27.8.1576)

frescoes. He did not remain in the city, however, though he always maintained a household there; in 1511 he moved to the Court of Padua, after 1516 to Ferrara and from 1523 he lived in Mantua. In 1533 he was elevated to the nobility and named as Court Painter. From 1543 he was a close friend of Pope Paul III. His most important patrons were the Emperor Charles V and his son Philip II of Spain. He died in Venice of the plague in 1576, according to some historians at the age of 86; others estimate his age as 91 or even 99.

In Venice his work can be seen in the Galleria dell'Accademia ("The Presentation of the Virgin", "St John the Baptist", "Pietà"), in the Chiesa dei Gesuiti ("Martyrdom of St Laurence"), in the Palazzo Ducale ("St Christophorus"), in the Church of Santa Maria dei Frari ("The Assumption of the Virgin", "Madonna of the Pesaro Family"), in the Church of San Salvatore ("The Annunciation") and in the Conti Collection ("St George").

Paolo Veronese
(Paolo Caliari)
(1528–19.4.1588)

As his name implies, Veronese was born in Verona, nevertheless he ranks with Tintoretto and Titian as one of the great artists of Venice in the Late Renaissance.

After working in 1552 on Mantua Cathedral, his home from 1554 was in Venice. Certain ambiguities in his "The Last Supper" actually brought him into conflict with the Inquisition but he made changes and characteristically retitled the painting "The Supper in the House of Levi". He was only able to complete all his commissions with the aid of a large studio and many assistants who transformed his drawings into paintings that reproduced his style.

His canvases are compositions on a grand scale that, with their gods and buffoons, monkeys, Moors and other exotic subjects, achieve a joyous splendour of sumptuous magnificence.

In Venice his works can be seen in the Church of San Sebastiano (ceiling- and wall-frescoes), in the Galleria dell'Accademia ("The Supper in the House of Levi") and in the Doges' Palace (ceiling- and wall-frescoes).

Antonio Vivaldi
(4.3.1678–28.7.1741)

Not only was Vivaldi Venice's most important composer, he also, through his development of the solo concerto, made a substantial contribution to European music.

In 1703 Vivaldi entered the priesthood and from that time worked intermittently until 1740 as a violin teacher, conductor and composer in the Ospedale della Pietà in Venice. He ranked as one of the greatest violinists of his time. He was highly thought of by Johann Sebastian Bach who, without asking his permission (which was not so unusual at that time), transposed several of Vivaldi's violin works for the organ, needless to say under his own name.

After centuries of neglect Vivaldi's work, of which some 770 pieces are known today, was rediscovered in 1926.

History of Venice

An Illyrian people, the Veneti, successfully settle as farmers and traders in the Upper Adriatic. — About 1000 B.C.

The Veneti are annexed into the Roman Empire; Padua becomes the wealthiest city in the Imperium Romanum after Rome. — 190 B.C.

Beginning of the great migrations when the Huns sweep into Europe. — A.D. 375

Division of the Empire by Theodosius into the Western Roman Empire (capital Ravenna) and the Eastern Roman Empire (capital Byzantium). — 395

The Veneti are forced to flee from Attila and his Huns into the swampland of the lagoon. — 452

Final destruction of the Western Roman Empire. Theodoric the Great founds an Ostrogothic Kingdom in Italy. — 476

End of the Gothic Kingdom; the troops of Justinian, the Eastern Roman Emperor, under their Commander Narses, occupy the lagoons. The cities of Venetia are placed under the Eastern Roman tribunes. — 553

The Langobards take possession of all of Northern Italy. The Veneti finally settle on the islands in the lagoon. Their territory continues to belong to the Eastern Roman Empire. — 568

Election of the first Doge (Latin "dux"=leader). He is Pauluccio Anafesto who governs from the island of Heraclea. — 697

During his rule Doge Teodato Ipato makes his seat the town of Malamocco on the Lido. — 742–755

Charlemagne conquers the Lombard Kingdom. His son, Pepin, makes an ineffectual attempt to capture the Venetian islands. The Venetians forsake Malamocco to retreat behind barricades on "Rivus Altus". The lagoon eventually stays in the Eastern Roman Empire and as a reward the Emperor in Constantinople grants the Venetians the status of a kind of Free State with an elected Doge at its head. Rivus Altus is built upon while the other island towns, Torcello and Malamocco, go into decline. The city is initially called "Civitas Venetiarum" and finally simply "Venetia". — 809

With the Treaty of Aachen between Charlemagne and the Eastern Roman Emperor Michael I the Venetians obtain greater independence from Byzantium. — 810

Venetian adventurers carry off the bones of the Apostle Mark from Alexandria to the Rialto, thus giving the Venetian State, which now calls itself the State of "San Marco", its own Patron Saint. — About 829

History of Venice

About 1000	Venice demands true independence from Constantinople, allies itself with the German Emperors, at that time Kings of Italy, and builds up its own empire. Venice conquers Istria and Dalmatia, sets up trading-posts throughout the Mediterranean and commands the greatest and most effective fleet in the Mediterranean.
1172	With the eventual introduction of the Great Council the constitution of the Republic is established, thus ensuring the hegemony of the nobility until the end of the Republic.
1177	Venice as Italy's Third Power concludes peace with Emperor Barbarossa and Pope Alexander III who thus proclaim the lagoon city an equal partner.
1202	Under the leadership of Doge Enrico Dandolo, blind and aged 92, Venice leads the ships of the Fourth Crusade which is persuaded to voyage to Constantinople instead of Palestine and to conquer the Eastern Roman Empire.
1204	After the conquest of Constantinople and the victory over Eastern Rome the Venetians keep for themselves three-eighths of the captured territory and Venice makes itself indispensable to the "Latin Empire" set up by the Crusaders in Constantinople. Venice is the master of trade throughout the Eastern Mediterranean and a World Power.
1210	Beginning of the war with Genoa, Venice's rival city state for supremacy in the Levantine trade.
1380	After 170 years of fighting Venice finally achieves naval superiority over Genoa. It is now the absolute centre of world trade.
1389–1484	Venice expands on the mainland and conquers the territory of Lombardy almost as far as Milan. It calls its mainland possessions "Terra firma".
1423	The city has a population of 200,000, and commands a fleet of over 45 galleys, 300 large and 3,000 medium-sized trading vessels, with a total complement of almost 40,000 seamen. Venice is by far the richest city in the West.
1453	The Turks conquer Constantinople and thus commences the slow decline of Venice as a World Power.
1492	With the discovery of America by Columbus predominance in world trade gradually shifts from Venice to Lisbon, London and the Low Countries.
1508	The Papal States led by Pope Julius II, unite with Spain, France and Germany against Venice in the League of Cambrai. The struggle weakens the city state.
1519	End of the fighting with the League, leaving the city utterly exhausted, financially and politically but managing to retain a good many of its conquests.

Venice once again controls the Peloponnese. The city is wealthy and a centre of banking.	1684–1718
In the Treaty of Passarowitz Venice cedes most of its trading-posts in the Levant to the Ottoman Empire.	1718
Napoleon I conquers the Republic of San Mark, without meeting any opposition. The city is separated from the surrounding territory.	1797
The city belongs to the Napoleonic Kingdom of Italy.	1805
Venice falls to Austria.	1815
In an uprising the Venetians, led by Daniele Manin, succeed in obtaining 15 months of independence. The rebellion is put down by General Radetzky of Austria.	1848–49
Venice is incorporated into the new Kingdom of Italy.	1866
Giuseppe Roncalli, Patriarch of Venice, becomes Pope John XXIII.	1958
The statesmen of the Western World meet in Venice for the international economic summit.	1980
In October the 35 signatories to the final communique of the Conference on European Security and cooperation, held in Helsinki in 1975, together with Israel and Egypt, hold an international conference to promote closer cooperation between Mediterranean countries.	1984

Quotations

"Streets full of water. Please advise."
(Telegram on arriving in Venice.)

Robert Benchley
American humorist

"Underneath Day's azure eyes
Ocean's nursling, Venice lies,
A peopled labyrinth of walls."

Percy Bysshe Shelley
(1792–1822)

"Venice is like eating an entire box of chocolate liqueurs at one go."

Truman Capote
American writer
"Observer", 1961

"Once did she hold the gorgeous East in fee,
And was the safeguard of the West: the worth
Of Venice did not fall below her birth,
Venice, the eldest child of liberty.
She was a maiden city, bright and free;
No guile seduced, no force could violate;
And when she took unto herself a mate,
She must espouse the everlasting sea.
And what if she had seen those glories fade,
Those titles vanish, and that strength decay,
Yet shall some tribute of regret be paid
When her long life hath reached its final day:
Men are we, and must grieve when even the shade
Of that which once was great has passed away."

William Wordsworth

"The State is all; it is for the individual unconditionally to serve the State. No one person may rise above the others, no cult of personality will be tolerated."

Constitution of the Republic

27

Quotations

Albrecht Dürer

J. W. von Goethe

Thomas Mann

Sposalizio del Mare (Wedding with the Sea)	"Desposamus te mare, in signum veri perpetuique dominii" – "O sea, we wed thee as a sign of true and everlasting dominion."
Count Avaux French Ambassador (mid 17th c.)	"It seems to me less difficult to have established this city on the face of the bottomless waters than to have united and led so many spirits in the same direction and despite the differing inclinations by which they are moved as individuals to have maintained the corporate body of this Republic, its power intact and unshaken."
Marino da Canala (1267)	"Goods circulate around this splendid city like the streams of water that spring from the fountain."
Cassiodorus (c. 490–580)	"The territory of Venetia is bordered in the South by the eminence of Ravenna and by the Po, in the East by the smiling cities of the Ionian coast. Here the tides suddenly retreat to reveal the changing face of the flooded land then flow back to cover it again. Your dwellings are built, like sea-birds' nests, half on sea and half on land, spread, as the Cyclades, over the surface of the waters. Through manmade earthworks you know how to bind your dwellings together. You heap up the sand to break the force of the raging waters and your walls, seemingly fragile, brave the force of the flood."
Philippe de Commynes French Ambassador (c. 1495)	"It is the finest highway to be found in the whole world, lined by the finest houses, and it passes through the whole of the city. The houses are very lofty and grand and of good stone and the older ones are painted over all, and they have stood there a hundred years. The others that have been built in the last century have façades of white marble that comes from Istria and of porphyry. Inside they all have no less than two chambers with gilded panels, rich chimneypieces of hewn marble and beds with gilded posts and the other chambers are also gilded and painted and furnished very well within. It is the most triumphant street I have ever seen, it is the most joyous city I ever saw."
Albrecht Dürer (21.5.1471–6.4.1528) German artist	(On the subject of the painter Bellini following Dürer's stay in Venice): "Giambellini, he that had already praised me to diverse gentlemen, he was most desirous to have something of me and

is himself come to me and begged me that I should make something for him, vouchsafing that he would make payment for it."

"It was written, then, on my page in the Book of Fate that at five in the afternoon of the twenty-eighth day of September in the year 1786, I should see Venice for the first time as I entered this beautiful island-city, this beaver-republic. . . . I have found comfortable lodgings . . . not far from the Piazza San Marco. My windows look out on to a narrow canal between high houses; immediately below them is a single-span bridge, and opposite, a narrow crowded passage. This is where I shall live until my parcel for Germany is ready and I have had my fill of sightseeing, which may be some time."

Johann Wolfgang
von Goethe
(28.8.1749–22.3.1832)
German poet
"Italian Journey"

"They sing in the squares, on the streets and on the canals. The vendors sing as they cry their wares, the workers sing as they leave their workplaces, the gondoliers sing as they wait for custom."

Carlo Goldoni
(25.2.1707–6.3.1793)
Italian playwright

"He saw it once more, that most astounding of landing-places, that breathtaking composition of fantastic buildings, which the Republic ranged to meet the awed gaze of the approaching seafarer; the airy splendour of the palace and the Bridge of Sighs, the columns of lion and saint on the shore, the glory of the projecting flank of the Basilica of St Mark, the vista of gateway and great clock. Looking, he thought that to come to Venice by the station is like entering a palace by the back door. No one should approach, save by the high seas as he was doing now, this most improbable of cities."

Thomas Mann
(6.6.1875–12.8.1955)
German author
"Death in Venice"

(On St Mark's Square):
"The most beautiful drawing-room in Europe, for which it is only fitting that the heavens should serve as a ceiling."

Napoleon Bonaparte
(15.8.1769–5.5.1821)
Emperor of France

"A city which is rich in gold, but richer still in fame and renown, which garners its strength from its armies and its trade but still more from the virtues of its people; which is founded on solid marble but is yet more secure upon the foundations of the unswerving unity of its population, and which, better than by the sea, is protected and safeguarded by the sagacity and the wisdom of its offspring."

Francesco Petrarca
i.e. Petrarch
(20.7.1304–18.7.1374)
Italian poet

"Venice is not only a special city, unlike any other in Italy, but it is also a special region, differing from any other region of Italy, with its own soil, its own sky, its own climate and its own air."

Hippolyte Taine
(21.4.1828–5.3.1893)
French philosopher

"As I was returning home late one night on the gloomy canal, the moon appeared suddenly and illuminated the marvellous palaces and the tall figure of my gondolier towering above the stern of the gondola, slowly moving his huge sweep. Suddenly he uttered a deep wail, not unlike the cry of an animal; the cry gradually gained in strength, and formed itself, after a long-drawn 'Oh!' into the simple musical exclamation 'Venezia!' This was followed by other sounds of which I have no distinct recollection, as I was so much moved at the time. Such were the impressions that to me appeared the most characteristic of Venice during my stay there, and they remained with me until the completion of the second act of 'Tristan', and possibly even suggested to me the long-drawn wail of the shepherd's horn at the beginning of the third act."

Richard Wagner
(22.5.1813–13.2.1883)
German composer

Venice from A to Z

Accademia (Academy)

See Galleria dell'Accademia

Ala Napoleonica (Napoleonic Wing)   K5

Location
Piazza di San Marco

The W side of the Piazza di San Marco (see entry) is formed by the Ala Napoleonica, which was built in 1810 by order of Napoleon I.
The work was entrusted to the architect Giuseppe Soli who simply copied the two lower floors of the Procuratie Nuove (see entry), omitted the third floor in order not to spoil the proportions of the Procuratie Vecchie, and topped his building with a heavy attic fronted by statues to bring it up to the height of the Procuratie Vecchie. The Ala Napoleonica contains the entrance to the Museo Correr (see entry).

Arsenale (Arsenal)   N/O/P4/5

Location
Rio del Arsenale

Quay
Arsenale

The Arsenal was Venice's shipyard – until the end of the 17th c. the largest and busiest in the world. Founded in 1104, it was continuously expanded and in its heyday employed as many as 4,000 workmen. The Arsenal was a prohibited area and accessible by one land and one sea approach only. Every workman was privy to its secrets and, therefore, subject to security checks, which was how the Republic managed to keep its art of shipbuilding secret until about 1550.
The entire Arsenal is still a closed military area without public access.
The landward entrance (Ingresso di Terra) is a triumphal arch in the Renaissance style. The lions on each side of the entrance come from Greece, booty brought back by Francesco Morosoni in the 17th c. after the reconquest of the Peloponnese. Of the two lions on the left, the larger one stood guard over the port of Piraeus while its fellow stood on the road from Athens to Eleusis.

** Basilica di San Marco (Basilica of St Mark)   K/L5

Location
Piazza di San Marco

The Basilica of St Mark was the spiritual centre of the Republic: a splendid building for the Patron Saint of the Republic, the church of the Doge and State.

Quay
San Marco

Originally the palace chapel of the Doge, it became important in 829 when the remains of St Mark were transferred to Venice from Alexandria and interred in the Capella di San Marco, which 150 years later, in 976, was destroyed by fire but soon rebuilt. Its present ground-plan, which is derived from the Church of the Apostles at Constantinople, dates from 1063 and consists of a Greek cross, covered by five domes, with two side aisles on the W arm pointing towards the Piazza di San Marco (see entry). In 1094 the basilica was consecrated in the presence of the Emperor Henry IV and some 744 years later were to pass before it became the Cathedral Church of Venice in 1807.

Three Procurators were appointed "Custodians of St Mark" to supervise the building and maintenance (see Procuratie). In the following centuries they supervised structural alterations to the basilica and its decoration: the mosaics were done in the 12th and 13th c. The 13th c. also saw the raising of the outer domes, the construction of the portico on the façade, the vaulting of the W porch, the installation of the bronze horses and the addition of the Byzantine parts of the Pala d'Oro. In the 14th c. the upper part of the façade and the domes were decorated in Gothic fashion and the pulpits and the Baptistery constructed. Further embellishments followed in the 15th–16th c. (altars, font, mosaics) and in the 17th–19th c. (mosaics).

The whole of Venice was legally compelled to take part in the rich furnishing of the State church: in 1075 the Doge Domenico Selvo passed a law that obliged all returning ships to bring back something precious to decorate the "House of St Mark", which is why today the basilica boasts over 500 columns of rare marble, porphyry, alabaster and jasper brought back from the East and Asia Minor.

The interior is clad with 4,240 sq. m (45,622 sq. ft) of gold mosaics, mostly 12th/13th c. Between 1500 and 1750, however, some of the venerable old sections were replaced by "modern" mosaics designed by artists including Titian and Tintoretto.

N façade

Exterior

This façade, facing the Piazzetta dei Leoncini, in the last arch contains the Porta dei Fiori, the Door of the Flowers, which merits close examination; its relief depicts the Nativity (13th c.), framed by foliage, angels and Prophets.

Also worth noting are two other reliefs (towards the Piazza): the Etoimasia (7th–8th c.) depicts the throne of the Judge with six sheep on each side (symbolising the Twelve Apostles). The other relief depicts Alexander the Great whose chariot is being drawn upwards by two griffins (10th c.).

W façade

The main façade on the Piazza is divided into five huge doorways. Over the portals is a terrace with a balustrade and above that five blind arches decorated with mosaics, topped by the Evangelists in gilded towers, Late Gothic ornamentation and figures. Above the central arch the so-called "Angel Staircase" leads up to the Patron Saint, St Mark. Behind the façade are the lead-covered domes.

The most remarkable of the mosaics decorating the portals is the one in the portal on the extreme left which dates from the 13th c. and depicts the Translation of the Body of St Mark to the Basilica.

The other mosaics are from the 17th and 18th c., and the Last Judgment over the centre portal dates only from 1836.

The central arch and the panels of the doors are richly decorated with reliefs and sculptures.

Piazzetta di San Marco with the Palazzo Ducale and Basilica di San Marco

San Marco: mosaic of the Last Judgment over the central portal

Gallery
Until 1981 the four world-famous bronze horses stood on the gallery. The horses were once part of a quadriga in the Hippodrome (ancient racecourse) of Constantinople. The date of their origin is still questionable; formerly they were thought to be the work of the 4th or 3rd c. B.C. (sculpted by Lysippos?). Recent research of British scientists ascribes them to the 3rd or 4th c. A.D. In 1204 they formed part of the booty brought to Venice by the Doge Enrico Dandolo after the fall of Constantinople. In 1797 Napoleon carried them off to Paris and they were returned to Venice in 1815. They can now be seen in the Museo Marciano.

Pietra del Bando
This "Stone of Banishment" at the SW corner of the façade is another spoil of conquest: from this stump of a porphyry column the decrees of the Republic were promulgated.

Flagpoles
The three huge cedar flagpoles in front of the façade were erected here in 1376 and their rich bronze bases were cast by Alessandro Leopardi in 1505.
The base of the middle flagpole has reliefs depicting Justice, Strength (an elephant) and Plenty. The southern flagpole base represents Venice's hegemony on land and the northern one represents the Republic's hegemony at sea.

S façade
Until 1503, when this façade was enclosed, it was intended to be an imposing ceremonial entrance facing the lagoon, with a large door leading into the atrium (left) and the Baptistery (right).
Besides the two griffins (in the first arch) it is worth noting a Byzantine mosaic of the Virgin (13th c.) between the arches of the upper floor, in front of which nowadays two lamps are kept burning; at the time of the Republic black tallow candles were lit to comfort those under sentence of death who were executed in front of the Colonne di Marco e Teodoro (see entry) on the Molo.

Pilastri Acritani
In front of the façade are two marble pilasters with magnificent reliefs (6th c.).). Also, the spoils of war, these were carried off by the Venetians in 1256 from the port of Acre.

Tetrarchs
The sculpture of the "Tetrarchs" (on the corner adjoining the Doge's Palace) is also world-famous. It was hewn from porphyry, probably in Egypt in the 4th c. and is thought to depict the Tetrarchs, Diocletian, Maximilian, Constantius and Valerius, who together ruled the Roman Empire in A.D. 285.

Like all Byzantine basilicas St Mark's has a porch (narthex).   Porch
The mosaics of the domes and arches are 13th c. (1220–1300); the only later addition was the "St Mark" inserted in the vaulting above the portal recess in 1545. Starting near the Zen Chapel and going N they depict the Creation, the story of Cain and Abel, the Building of Noah's Ark, the Building of the Tower of Babel, the story of Abraham, of Joseph and of Moses.

Basilica di San Marco

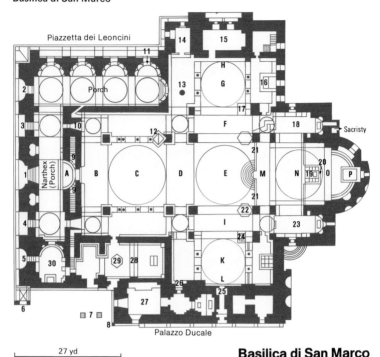

Piazzetta dei Leoncini

Porch

Narthex (Porch)

Sacristy

Palazzo Ducale

27 yd
25 m

Basilica di San Marco

The **Basilica di San Marco** was begun in 830, rebuilt in 976 after a fire and remodelled in the 11th c. on the Byzantine pattern. The building inside measures 76·5 m (240·9 ft) by 51·8 m (169·9 ft) and is in the shape of a Greek cross. It has five domes. The interior is impressive for the beauty of its architecture, the changing views through the building and the magnificent mosaics.

1 Main portal
2–5 Portal recesses
6 Pietra del Bando
7 Pilastri Acritani
8 Sculpture of the Tetrarchs
9 Stairs up to the Museo Marciano
10 Porta di San Pietro
11 Porta dei Fiori
12 Capitello del Crocifisso (Capital of the Cross)
13 Romanesque stoup with angels (12th c.)
14 Cappella della Madonna dei Mascoli
15 Cappella di Sant'Isidoro
16 Cappella della Madonna Nicopeia

17 Altare di San Pietro
18 Cappella di San Pietro
19 High Altar
20 Pala d'Oro
21 Iconostasis
22 Reliquary
23 Cappella di San Clemente
24 Altare di San Giacomo
25 Passage to the Doges' Palace
26 Entrance to the Treasury
27 Tesoro (Treasury), with goldsmiths' work, etc.
28 Battistero (Baptistery)
29 Font dating from 1546
30 Cappella Zen, named after Cardinal G. B. Zen (d. 1501)

MOSAICS
A Arch of Paradise
B Arch of the Apocalypse
C Scenes of Pentecost
D Scenes from the Passion
E The Ascension
F St Michael with sword
G St John
H Mary's family tree
I The Washing of the Feet, Temptation in the Wilderness
K St Leonard
L Four miracles of Jesus
M St Peter, The Resurrection, etc.
N Choir mosaics
O Lamb of God
P Christ in Majesty, with Saints

Three portals lead to the interior of the church. All three are flanked by marble columns with richly ornamented capitals (6th–9th c.). The left portal shows Abraham with the three angels; the right portal has a bronze door covered in silver with an inscription in Greek (10th c.).

The middle portal, Venetian 12th c. work, was the main entrance to the church until 1064.

In the outer wall of the narthex are 12th c. tombs of Doges.

The basic shape of the Basilica di San Marco is Byzantine, yet it is an astonishing mixture of styles containing elements of nearly every architectural form from Classical to 19th c. Its form of building and its art treasures, acquired by such a diversity of means, have made the Basilica di San Marco one of the most important works of art in the world.

Interior of the Basilica

Four huge pillars bearing the domes and six columns with gilded capitals divide it into a nave and two aisles. Each of the five domes is almost 13 m (43 ft) in diameter and has 16 windows. The sumptuous mosaics that cover the domes (over a total surface area of 4,240 sq. m (45,622 sq. ft)) fully justify its being popularly known as the "Basilica d'Oro" (Golden Basilica).

Domes

Before beginning to look round the church it is worth pausing to look at the dome mosaics, most of which date from between 1160 and 1200. Their chronological order begins in the E (above the choir), runs above the nave and finishes in the domes in the transept. The best view of the mosaics is from the galleries (anyone who is especially interested should go armed with a telescope or binoculars). Access is from the inner portal.

Emanuel Dome
Christ giving a blessing and surrounded and venerated by Mary and the Prophets.

Ascension Dome (centre)
Christ surrounded by stars; below, Mary between two cherubim and the Apostles.

Pentecost Dome
The dove of the Holy Ghost is in the centre of a halo that extends to the Apostles round the edge of the dome: it symbolises the Holy Ghost entering into the Disciples.

Cappella di San Giovanni (N transept)
It has mosaics showing the life of St John (1180).

Dome of St Leonard (S transept)
Mosaics depicting SS Leonard, Clement, Blasius and Nicholas (13th c.). The basilica had altars dedicated to these four saints.

Columned aedicula
The hexagonal columned aedicula has a pyramidal marble roof crowned by precious Oriental agate.
Another treasure is the Byzantine Crucifix from Constantinople.

Tour (clockwise)

Capella della Madonna dei Máscoli
The Chapel of the Madonna dei Máscoli is so named because it became the chapel of an all-male confraternity in 1618. It has

a fine stoup (12th c.) and Gothic altar sculptures dating from 1430 by Bartolomeo Bon. The mosaics of 1430–50 on the barrel-vault depict the Life of the Virgin. "The Birth of the Virgin" and "The Presentation" on the left wall bear the signature of Michele Giambono and are emphatically Gothic whereas "The Visitation" and "The Dormition of the Virgin" on the right wall close to the style of Jacopo Bellini are the earliest examples of the Renaissance in Venice.

Cappella di Sant'Isidoro
The remains of the Saint were acquired by the unusual form of purchase in Chios in 1125 and interred in this chapel. The wall sarcophagus and the mosaics (mid 14th c.) depicting the life of St Isidore are worth seeing.

Cappella della Madonna Nicopeia
The most valuable item of decoration of the altar on the E side of the transept is the Byzantine icon of the Madonna Nicopeia ("the Bearer of Victory"). The icon, set with jewels, pearls and precious stones and in a delicate Byzantine enamel frame, was booty from Constantinople in 1204. The Madonna is greatly venerated by the Venetians.

Cappella di San Pietro
From the chapel there is a good view of the choir and the High Altar and of the mosaics in the arches on the opposite side.

Access
Cappella di San Clemente

Admission charge

Rood-screen
In front of the choir (near the sacramental altar) is the intricate rood-screen. The lectern with the silver Crucifix and the statues of the Madonna, of St Mark and the Apostles was the work of Jacopello and Pierpaolo dalle Massegne (1394–1404). The rood-screen pulpit (right) was where the newly elected Doge was traditionally presented to the people.

Presbytery
The Presbytery was where the clergy, the Doge and the highest officials of Venice met on holy days (the basilica was a city church). The Doge's seat is no longer present, however, and the original stalls have been replaced.

Choir platforms
The bronze reliefs by Jacopo Sansovino (1537–41), show scenes from the story of St Mark.

High Altar
The High Altar (1834–36) houses the relics of St Mark. Of interest are the four columns supporting the baldachin which are decorated with 324 reliefs showing scenes from the life of Jesus and Mary.

Opening times
Summer: Mon.–Sat. 10 a.m.– 5 p.m., Sun. 2–4.30 p.m.; Winter: Mon.–Sat. 9.30 a.m.–4.30 p.m., Sun. 2– 4.30 p.m.

Admission charge

Pala d'Oro
San Marco's golden retable is the work of Byzantine and Venetian goldsmiths and enamellers who worked on it for 500 years. It is 3·45 m (11·32 ft) long and 1·4 m (4·6 ft) high.
The oldest sections are the circular gold and enamel plates on the rim (c. 976).
The enamel plates with episodes from the story of St Mark and scenes from the New Testament (1105) are Venetian.
The six large scenes from the life of Jesus (1209) are Byzantine.

Mosaics in San Marco

Pala d'Oro

Tetrarchs embracing

The middle panel with the figure of Christ in Majesty, the medallions with the Evangelists, the Twelve Apostles and the frame are also Venetian (13th c.).

Sacristy
The bronze door to the Sacristy is a masterpiece by Jacopo Sansovino (1486–1570). The reliefs show The Resurrection (top), The Entombment (bottom) and Saints and Prophets (at the edges). The heads are thought to be those of the artists Titian, Aretino, Palladio, Veronese and the Sansovino brothers.

Cappella di San Clemente
Noteworthy features in the former chapel of the Doge are the dividing wall of columns (late 14th c.), the mosaic of St Clement in the apse (12th c.) and the Holy Virgin on the altar.

Sacramental altar
The altar as made in1617. In front of it is the spot (marked by a mosaic in the floor) where the relics of St Mark were rediscovered after they had been lost in the fire of 976.

Opening times
Summer: Mon.–Sat. 10 a.m.–
5 p.m.; Sun. 2–4.30 p.m.;
Winter: Mon.–Fri. 9.30 a.m.–
4.30 p.m., Sun. 2–4.30 p.m.

Admission charge

Tesoro
The Treasury is full of the precious objects brought to Venice by the Venetians after the Sack of Constantinople in 1204 and which formed the basis of the now world-famous Treasure of San Marco.
Among the valuable objects captured in Constantinople were 110 Byzantine reliquaries made of gold and silver and set with precious stones (11th–13th c. work), Byzantine liturgical items, Byzantine icons made of gold and silver with reliefs, and the traditional "Seat of St Mark" (c. 630). The sumptuous throne of the Doges (1500) is one of the few objects on display not brought to Venice as booty captured in war.

Battistero
The mosaics (14th c.) on the ceiling of the Baptistery depict the sending out of the Apostles ("Go out into the world and baptise all the peoples") and those on the walls show scenes from the Life of St John the Baptist.
The font, thought to be by Sansovino, has bronze reliefs also showing the Life of St John the Baptist. The figure of the Apostle comes from Segala (1556). Opposite the entrance is the tomb of Andrea Dandolo, the last Doge to be buried in San Marco.

Cappella Zen
The chapel houses the Tomb of Cardinal Giambattista Zen. The bronze Madonna (1515) between St Mark and St John, called the "Madonna with the shoe", is outstanding. According to the legend a poor man presented the Madonna with his left shoe which then turned to gold as a sign of heavenly gratitude.
The two red marble lions (c. 1200), Lombardy work, are also of interest.
The chapel was originally a room opening on to the Piazzetta and the main entrance in the S façade.

Museo Marciano

The Museo Marciano (Museum of St Mark) is the museum of the basilica. It has magnificent 13th–16th c. tapestries, 12th c.

Byzantine sculptures and a very fine cover for the Pala d'Oro made in 1345 by Paolo Veneziano showing scenes from the Life of St Mark. The four gilded copper horses, previously on the gallery of San Marco, are now in the museum.
There is an admission charge.

Opening times
Summer: 9.30 a.m.–
5.30 p.m. daily; Winter
9.30 a.m.–4 p.m. daily

Burano (island)

The pretty little fishing village with painted houses and boats has been very well restored and is now the lagoon's artists' colony.
Burano lace is famous: it is not made on bobbins but stitched. This art had been almost forgotten before it was revived in the early years of the 20th c.
The Palazzo del Podestà (14th c.) contains the Scuola dei Merletti (Lace School) and a small museum with particularly fine pieces from various centuries (closed on Tuesdays).

Quay
Burano (from Fondamenta Nuove)

*Ca' Foscari   G5

The palace, today part of the university, is one of Venice's most important Late Gothic buildings. When Doge Francesco Foscari (1423–57) ordered its building in the 15th c. it had four floors which was unheard of.
Foscari enlarged the mainland of the Venetian Republic in the West but neglected to formulate policy in the East and was eventually forced in 1454 to sign a declaration surrendering the Eastern Mediterranean to the Turkish Sultan. In 1457, the year of his death, Fascari was overthrown by his opponents, the Loredani family, and his son Jacopo was banished.
In 1574 King Henry III of France used the palace as a residence.
The main façade overlooks the Canal Grande.

Location
Rio di Ca' Foscari/
Canal Grande

Quay
Ca' Rezzonico

*Ca' da Mosto   K4

The palace dates back to the 12th c. and was built in the Venetian-Byzantine style. Alvise da Mosto, the first European to sail round Cape Verde in West Africa in 1465, was born in this house in 1432. Between the 16th and the 18th c. the Ca' da Mosto housed the well-known Leon Bianco (White Lion) Hotel. In 1769 and 1775 the German Emperor and son of Maria Theresa, Joseph II, lived here during his stay in Venice.
The main façade overlooks the Canal Grande.

Location
Calle Postal/Canal Grande

Quay
Ca' d'Oro

*Ca' d'Oro with the Galleria Franchetti (Golden House)   J3

This palace is Venetian Gothic at its most perfect. Originally richly painted and gilded – hence its name – it has lost its gilding but the marble filigree-work of Bartolomeo Bon (who also built the Porta della Carta in the Palazzo Ducale (see entry)) dating from between 1421 and 1440 is still of unrivalled beauty. The

Location
Canal Grande

Quay
Ca' d'Oro

Opening times
Tues.–Sat. 9 a.m.–2 p.m.
Sun., public holidays 9 a.m.–
1 p.m. closed Mon.

interior provides a vivid impression of how Venetian nobles lived in the late Middle Ages. The mosaic on the ground floor, a copy of the one in the basilica of Saint Mark, is also worth seeing.

There is a red marble well in the courtyard with allegories of Strength, Justice and Mercy.

The palace houses the Galleria Franchetti art collection, given to the State in 1922 by the saviour of the Ca' d'Oro, Baron Giorgio Franchetti. Extensive restoration work (1969–84) has not altered the character of the private collection. The exhibits do not give the impression of being in a museum, but rather complement the historical setting of the palace.

First floor (Rooms 1–6): magnificent 15th c. staircase; "Venus and Cupid" by Paris Bordone (16th c.); "The Annunciation and Death of the Virgin" by Carpaccio (c. 1500); four bronze reliefs by Riccio (c. 1510); beautiful 16th c. furniture and tapestries; sculptures; Titian's famous "Venus before the Mirror"; lovely 16th c. golden decorated ceiling (Room 4); "Madonna" by a pupil of Bellini (1500); unfinished "St Sebastian" by Mantegna (c. 1500).

Second floor (Rooms 7–18): painting by Bonifacio Pitati; "Portrait of a Nobleman" by Van Dyck (1622–27); Tuscan paintings; collection of medals; small Italian bronzes; Flemish paintings.

The main façade overlooks the Canal Grande.

---

* Ca' Venier dei Leoni e Raccolta Peggy Guggenheim   H/J6
(Venier House of the Lions and Peggy Guggenheim Collection)

Location
Canal Grande/
Fondamenta Venier

Quay
Salute, Accademia

Opening times
Mon., Wed.–Sun. noon–
6 p.m.; Sat. also 6–9 p.m.
(Apr.–Oct.)

Closed
Tues. Nov.–March

Admission charge

The palace, only a few steps away from the Church of Santa Maria della Salute (see entry) and the Palazzo Corner della Ca' Grande (see entry), was begun in 1749. It was never completed, however, and has only one floor. The aristocratic Venier family are said to have kept lions in the sleepy garden – hence the appellation "dei Leoni" (of the Lions).

After the Second World War the American heiress Peggy Guggenheim (1898–1979) bought the building and filled it with her private collection of Abstract and Surrealist paintings and sculptures; apart from works by Jackson Pollock, whom she discovered, and Max Ernst, to whom she was married, her collection includes works by Alberto Giacometti, Vassily Kandinsky, Marc Chagall, Pablo Picasso, Paul Klee, Georges Braque, Emilio Vedova, Brancusi, Arp, Léger and Tanguy.

---

* Campanile   K5

Location
Piazza di San Marco

Quay
San Marco

Opening times
10 a.m.–7.30 p.m. daily.
Winter 10 a.m.–4 p.m.

Admission charge

The Piazza di San Marco (see entry) would not be complete without the rectangular towering Campanile in front of the Procuratie Nuove (see entry) that links the Piazza and the Piazzetta (see entry).

The Campanile was begun in the 10th c.; it was completed in the 12th c. and its pointed roof added in the 15th c. It could be seen from afar by approaching ships and it guided them home with its gilded pinnacle.

It collapsed on 14 July 1902, smashing the Loggetta (see entry) at its foot but causing no casualties. By 1912 it had been painstakingly rebuilt.

The Campanile is 98·6 m (322·6 ft) high and has a double wall.

Ca' d'Oro: Venetian architecture at its zenith

A lift goes up to the Belfry from where there is a magnificent view of the city.
In the Middle Ages the Campanile was also used as a pillory: wrongdoers – including adulterers and renegade priests – were closeted in a cage and hoisted half-way up the tower. This breezy punishment could last for several weeks.

I Carmini (officially: Santa Maria del Carmine; church) F5

The Gothic church with the tall 17th c. Campanile dates from the 13th to the 14th c. Like the Scuola dei Carmini (see entry), it belonged to the Carmelites.
The interior has some very fine paintings, several in the nave showing scenes from the history of the Order. The "Adoration of the Shepherds" (early 16th c.), one of Cima da Conegliano's most highly prized works, is at the second side-altar on the right and Lorenzo Lotto's "St Nicholas and Saints" (early 16th c.) is in the left-hand aisle.

Location
Campo Carmini

Quay
Ca' Rezzonico

Chiesa dell'Angelo Raffaele (Church of the Archangel Raphael) E6

This church was founded as early as the 7th c. but the present building which is rather austere dates from the 17th c.
Inside in the organ-loft is a series of pictures depicting the story of Tobias. These important 18th c. paintings are by one of the Guardi brothers, but it is not clear whether the artist was Giovanni Antonio Guardi or his younger brother Francesco.

Location
Campo San Sebastiano

Quay
Ca' Rezzonico

*Chiesa dei Gesuati (officially: Santa Maria del Rosario; church) G/H6

Location
Fondamenta Zattere dei
Gesuati

Quay
Accademia

In the 15th c. the church belonged to the Guild of the Poveri Gesuati (whose name it has retained) but was taken over by the Dominicans when the Guild was suppressed by Pope Clement IX in 1668. The Dominicans had the present building erected in 1726–36 by the master-builder Giorgio Massari. It is a gem of 18th c. Venetian architecture: a large room with side-chapels and a façade reminiscent of Palladio.

There are ceiling-frescoes by Giambattista Tiepolo – "The Ascent into Heaven of St Dominic", "The Introduction of the Rosary by Mary", "St Dominic giving a Blessing"; and the painting "Madonna in Glory".

The altar-piece "St Dominic" (*c.* 1473; second altar on the right) "Dominicans" (third altar on the right) are by Piazzetta; Sebastiano Ricci was responsible for the altar-piece "Pope Pius V and Saints" (*c.* 1732–34; first altar on the left) and Tintoretto painted "The Crucifixion" (third altar on the left).

*Chiesa degli Scalzi F3
(officially: Santa Maria di Nazareth; Church of the Discalced)

Location
Lista di Spagna

Quay
Ferrovia (railway station)

The church is a fine Baroque building and was built between 1670 and 1680 by Baldassare Longhena. Its façade was added between 1683 and 1689 by Giuseppe Sardi. The building is famed for its many sculptures. In the second chapel on the right is Tiepolo's fresco "The Glory of St Teresa", and the third chapel on the left contains his fresco "Christ praying in the garden of Gethsemane".

The ceiling-fresco by Tiepolo was destroyed by an Austrian grenade during the First World War. The present ceiling-fresco is the work of Ettore Tito (1934).

Colonne di Marco e Teodoro (Columns of St Mark and St Theodore) L5

Location
Molo

Quay
San Marco

Doge Michieli actually brought three columns back from Tyre (now in the Lebanon) in 1125 but when they were being unloaded one of them fell into the sea and sank to the bottom of the lagoon.

The other two were set up on the Molo. One of them was crowned with the Lion of St Mark – probably an early medieval mythical animal from Persia that had been given wings and a book between its paws. Until the 18th c. the lion was gilded. St Theodore was set up on the second column; he was the first Patron Saint of Venice until superseded by St Mark. The gleaming white statue has been skilfully assembled: the head belongs to a Roman Emperor and the rest, including the dragon, to an early St George.

Spectacular executions took place between the two columns, hence the belief that walking between them still brings bad luck.

Fondaco dei Tedeschi

Dogana di Mare (Old Customs House)   K6

The Customs House was built by G. Benoni between 1676 and 1682 when the Senate hoped they could halt the decline in the Venetian economy by enforcing rigorous customs regulations. On the tip of the spire is a weathervane of "Fortuna", seen standing on a gilded globe supported by two telamones.

Location
Punta della Dogana

Quay
Salute

Doges' Palace

See Palazzo Ducale

---

*Fondaco dei Tedeschi (German Commodity Exchange)   K4

The Fondaco (from the Arabic "funduk"=commodity exchange) dei Tedeschi, the German Commodity Exchange, is first recorded in 1228. At that time the "German" merchants also included Poles, Czechs and Hungarians. Today the building contains the main Post Office. When the Fondaco burned down in 1505 the Republic assumed the cost of rebuilding it and entrusted the decoration of the façade (and its vanished frescoes) to Giorgione and Titian.
This underlined the economic advantages which the republic obtained from this institution. On every purchase and sale –

Location
Ponte di Rialto
(access)

Quay
Rialto

these generally involved considerable sums – a high commission had to be paid to the state of Venice. In the 16th and 17th centuries the Fondaco was fittingly known as the "Golden ark of the senate". The importance of the exchange was illustrated by its location close to the Rialto; the commodity exchanges of other nations were unable to claim and maintain a similar favourable position. Only the Turkish exchange (see Fondaco dei Turchi) was located on the Grand Canal. The exchange was both a place of business and a refuge for the merchants. They were not permitted to appear alone, nor to conduct any business outside the Fondaco. They were subjected to strict controls, they lived and ate communally (no women were allowed) and they were subjected to Venetian supervision. Publically the German merchants were presented as a "brotherhood" of the Church of San Bartolomeo (see entry) which belonged to them.

The façade on the Canal Grande is, in accordance with Venetian tradition, in three sections. The middle section is a five-arched "Portico"; above this are the dining-rooms on the corners of the upper floor, topped by an ornamental merlon-like moulding.

The architecture of the building corresponds exactly to the purpose for which it served: 160 rooms are spread over four floors surrounding a courtyard. The shops were in the outer rooms of the ground floor while the other rooms were used for storage. The rooms of the upper floors were living-quarters and offices. The Customs post overlooked the canal.

* Fondaco dei Turchi e Museo di Storia Naturale   H3
(Turkish Commodity Exchange and Natural History Museum)

Location
Fondamenta del Megio/
Rio Fortego dei Turchi

Quay
San Staè

Opening times
Tues.–Sat. 9 a.m.–1.30 p.m.,
Sun., public holidays 9 a.m.–
noon

Closed
Mon.

Admission charge

The building, originally a palace, dates from the 9th c. and is one of the oldest in Venice. It has existed in its present form since the mid 13th c. In the 14th and 15th c. it was the residence in Venice of the Dukes of Ferrara. Emperor Friedrich III stayed here as their guest in 1452 and 1469.

From 1608 to 1621 the Emperor's Ambassador, Georg Fugger, had his office in this palace.

In 1621 the Council of the Republic allocated the building to the Turkish merchants for use as living accommodation and as a warehouse (hence the appellation "Fondaco"). At the beginning of the 19th c. the palace was totally in ruins, so the city took it over and after 1858 rebuilt it in its original 13th c. style; since 1880 it has been used as a museum and today is an outstanding example of the Byzantine-Venetian mixture of styles common in the 13th c.

The building currently houses the Natural History Museum (Museo di Storia Naturale).

The museum gives a good idea of the animal life in the Adriatic, but its impressive array of exhibits also covers other marine areas. The associated lapidary and general zoological collections are well worth seeing.

The ground floor also contains a notable exhibition of Venetian well-heads.

I Frari: Titian, "The Assumption of the Virgin" ("Assunta") ▶

Santa Maria Gloriosa dei Frari

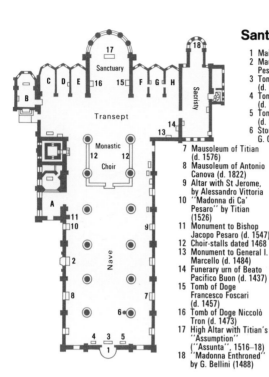

1 Main portal
2 Mausoleum of Doge Giovanni Pesaro (d. 1659)
3 Tomb of Girolamo Garzoni (d. 1688)
4 Tomb of Pietro Bernardo (d. 1538)
5 Tomb of Alvise Pasqualigo (d. 1528)
6 Stoup with statuettes by G. Campagna (1593)
7 Mausoleum of Titian (d. 1576)
8 Mausoleum of Antonio Canova (d. 1822)
9 Altar with St Jerome, by Alessandro Vittoria
10 "Madonna di Ca' Pesaro" by Titian (1526)
11 Monument to Bishop Jacopo Pesaro (d. 1547)
12 Choir-stalls dated 1468
13 Monument to General I. Marcello (d. 1484)
14 Funerary urn of Beato Pacifico Buon (d. 1437)
15 Tomb of Doge Francesco Foscari (d. 1457)
16 Tomb of Doge Niccolò Tron (d. 1473)
17 High Altar with Titian's "Assumption" ("Assunta", 1516–18)
18 "Madonna Enthroned" by G. Bellini (1488)

CHAPELS
A Emiliani
B Corner: marble statue of St John the Baptist (1554); altar-piece by Bartolomeo Vivarini (1474)
C Milanesi: grave-slab of Claudio Monteverdi (d. 1643); altar-piece by Alvise Vivarini
D Trevisan: (Tomb of Melchiorre Trevisan (d. 1500)
E San Francesco
F Fiorentini: wood-carving of St John the Baptist by Donatello (1451)
G Sacramento: wall tomb of the Florentine Ambassador, Duccio degli Alberti (d. 1336)
H Bernardo: polyptych by Bartolomeo Vivarini (1482)

I Frari (officially: Santa Maria Gloriosa dei Frari; church) **G4/5

Location
Campo San Rocco

Quay
San Tomà

Admission charge

Interior

This Gothic church was begun by the Franciscans ("Frari" in Venetian="Frati" in Italian) about 1340. The façade, interior, annexes, Cappella Emiliana and Cappella Cornaro were added in the middle of the 15th c. The simple unadorned interior corresponds to the ideals of the Franciscan monks. The impressive Campanile (14th c.) is the second highest in the city.

Among the church's outstanding works of art are:
N aisle
Mausoleum of A. Canova
The mausoleum was made by the pupils of the sculptor Antonio Canova (1757–1822). It contains only his heart, his body having been buried in Possagno, his native town.

Mausoleum of Doge Giovanni Pesaro
The mausoleum for Doge Giovanni Pesaro is the work of the sculptor Baldassare Longhena.

"Madonna di Ca' Pesaro"
This painting, completed in 1526, is one of Titian's most important works.

Cappella Emiliani
The chapel has a very fine polyptych with marble figures (mid 15th c.).

Left transept
Cappella Cornaro
The statue of St John the Baptist on the stoup was created by the sculptor and master-builder Jacopo Sansovino (c. 1550).

Cappella Milonesi
In this chapel is an inscribed stone marking the grave of Claudio Monteverdi (1567–1643), the pioneer of opera; the retable "St Ambrose with Saints" and "Coronation of the Virgin" was begun by Alvise Vivarini and completed by Marco Basaiti.

Sanctuary
The Sanctuary contains the tomb of the Doges Francesco Foscari (1423–47) and Niccolò Tron (1471–73) by Antonio Rizzo. Of especial note is Titian's painting, created between 1516 and 1518, over the High Altar, the "Assunta" (Assumption of the Virgin).

Right transept
Statue of St John the Baptist
The Florentine sculptor Donatello (c. 1386–1466) created this figure in wood in 1451 (first chapel to the right of the Sanctuary). It depicts St John the Baptist preaching – his mouth is open and his right hand raised in gesture.

Cappella Bernardo
In the third chapel to the right of the Sanctuary is a triptych by the Italian painter Bartolomeo Vivarini "Madonna with Child and Saints"; it dates from 1482.

The Sacristy
The triptych "The Madonna and Child Enthroned with four Saints". The painting, a gift from the Pesaro family, is by Giovanni Bellini. It depicts the Patron Saint of Pietro Pesaro (father), Niccolò, Marco and Benedetto (sons).

Nave
Monastic Choir
This is the only Monastic Choir in Venice left in its original position. The enclosure is by the Lombardo studio. The choir is an outstanding example of the wood-carving of Marco Cozzi.

S aisle
"St Jerome"
The marble statue by Alessandro Vittoria dates from 1560. The stone in the Saint's hand refers to his self-castigation. Jerome lived as a hermit for a time.

Mausoleum of Titian
This was a gift from Ferdinand I of Austria, king of Lombardy Veneto, and is the work of the Zandomeneghi brothers (1852).

Galleria dell'Accademia (Academy of Fine Arts)   H6

The Galleria dell'Accademia, called "Accademia" for short, is on the Canal Grande near the Ponte dell'Accademia (see entry). It has the most important and comprehensive collection of 15th–18th c. Venetian painting in existence.

Location
Canal Grande/Pora dell'Accademia (access)

Galleria dell'Accademia

Quay
Accademia

Opening times
Tues.–Sat. 9 a.m.–2 p.m.,
Sun., public holidays 9 a.m.–
1 p.m.

Closed
Mon.

Admission charge

The basis of the collection was the Accademia di Belle Arti founded in 1750 by the painter Giovanni Battista Piazzetta. Since 1807 it has been housed in the former Monastery of Santa Maria della Carità (1441), the Scuola di Santa Maria della Carità (15th c.) and the adjacent monastery buildings of the Lateran Canons (c. 1500).

Church, monastery and school were secularised about 1800. In 1802 private art-lovers set up a temporary depot in the empty rooms for works of art that had become "homeless" after the closure of monasteries and churches and the clearing of the palaces of noble families. In a very short time a unique gallery was assembled in this way, and was steadily enlarged by purchases and donations.

Room 1: This room formerly belonged to the Scuola di Santa Maria della Carità and has a richly carved and gilded ceiling (15th c.). It contains works by masters of Venetian Gothic painting such as Paolo Veneziano, Lorenzo Venesiano, Michele Giambono, Antonio Vivarini and Jacobello del Fiore.

Room 2: 15th and 16th c. Renaissance painting. "Madonna and Saints" by Giovanni Bellini (1430–1516), "The Garden of Gethsemane" by Marco Basaiti, "Portrait of Christ" by Vittore Carpaccio and "Madonna under the Orange Tree" by Cima da Conegliano.

Room 3: 16th c. Venetian panel-paintings.

Room 4: Paintings from the second half of the 15th c. "St George" by Andrea Mantegna, "St Jerome and a Donor" by Piero della Francesca, "Madonna and Child" by Cosmè Tura and works by Giovanni Bellini.

Room 5: "Sacra Conversazione" – also called "Madonna Giovanelli" – by Giovanni Bellini and five panels with allegories; works by the Venetian painter Giorgione: "Tempèsta" (probably the master's best-known work) and "Old Woman".

Room 6: "Fishermen presenting St Mark's Ring to the Doge" by Paris Bordone, "Banquet of Dives" by Bonifacio de' Pitati and "St John the Baptist" by Titian.

Room 7: "Gentleman in his Study" by the Venetian painter Lorenzo Lotto and "Portrait of a Lady" by Bernardo Licinio.

Room 8: Palma the Elder's "Sacra Conversazione".

Room 9: Paintings by Bonifacio de' Pitati and Fr. Vecellio and works by the school of Tintoretto.

Room 10: Scenes by Jacopo Tintoretto from the Life of St Mark, including "The Miracle of St Mark"; "Supper in the House of Levi" by Paolo Veronese and the magnificent "Pietà" by Titian.

Room 11: Several works by Jacopo Tintoretto, including "Cain and Abel"; "The Marriage of St Catherine" by Paolo Veronese and works by the Venetian painter Giambattista Tiepolo, and by Luca Giordano and Pietro da Cortona.

Room 12: 18th c. Italian landscapes.

Galleria dell'Accademia

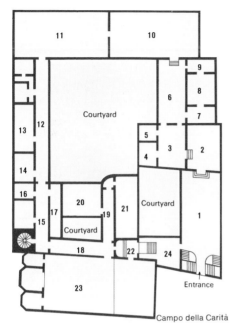

ROOMS
1 14th–15th c. panel-painting
2 15th–16th c. Venetian Renaissance altar-pieces
3 16th c. Venetian panel-paintings
4 Second half of 15th c.
5 G. Bellini, Giorgione
6 16th c. Venetian painting
7 Lorenzo Lotto, Bernardo Licinio
8 Palma the Elder
9 Bonifacio de' Pitati, Fr. Vecellio, school of Tintoretto.
10 16th c. Venetian masters including Veronese, Tintoretto and Titian
11 Tintoretto, Bassano, Tiepolo, Veronese, Giordano, Da Cortona
12 Corridor: 18th c. landscapes
13 16th c. Venetian painting
14 Early 17th c.
15 Corridor: Tiepolo, Pellegrini
16 18th c. Venetian painting
17 Small 18th c. paintings
18 18th c. paintings
19 19th c. panel-paintings
20 "Miracles of the Relic of the True Cross"
21 Vittore Carpaccio's "Legend of St Ursula"
22 Paintings from the first half of the 18th c.
23 Former monastery church: G. Bellini, A. and B. Vivarini, Cima da Conegliano
24 Former Hall of the Scuola della Carità: A. Vivarini, Titian, etc.

Room 13: Works by 16th c. Venetian and mainland painters including Jacopo Bassano and Jacopo Tintoretto.

Room 14: 17th c. Italian painters, including Bernardo Strozzi, Domenico Fetti and the German painter Johann Liss.

Room 15: Two paintings with religious themes by Giandomenico Tiepolo (son of Giambattista Tiepolo).

Rooms 16–19: Early works by Giambattista Tiepolo (18th c.), "The Fortune Teller" by Giovanni Battista Piazzetta (a major work), and paintings by Francesco Guardi and Giovanni Antonio Canaletto (see General Information, Prominent Figures in Venetian History). Genre-paintings by Pietronghi, pastel portraits by the Venetian-born Rosalba Carriera and models by Antonio Canova.

Room 20: This room contains paintings from the Scuola di San Giovanni Evangelista, including the work of Gentile Bellini, Vittore Carpaccio, Giovanni Mansueti, Lazzaro Bastiani, etc. All paintings relate to the miracles of the relic of the True Cross. This relic of the True Cross is still kept in the Scuola.

Room 21: A series of paintings of the legend of St Ursula by Vittore Carpaccio (late 15th c.).

Room 22: Corridor with Neo-Classical pictures.

Room 23: This room was part of the former Monastery Church of Santa Maria della Carità. It contains 15th and 16th c. paintings by G. Bellini, Alvise and Bartolomeo Vivarini, Cima da Conegliano, etc.

Room 24: Former Hall of the Scuola della Corità. It contains "The Presentation of the Virgin at the Temple" by Titian, "The Madonna Enthroned with Saints" by A. Vivarini, a large Triptych by Giovanni d'Alemagna, and a Byzantine-Venetian reliquary.

Galleria d'Arte Moderna

See Palazzo Pesaro

Galleria Franchetti

See Ca' d'Oro

*I Gesuiti (officially: Santa Maria Assunta; church)   K/L3

Location
Campo Gesuiti

Quay
Ca' d'Oro

The church dating from the 13th c. was sumptuously rebuilt between 1714 and 1729 by Domenico Rossi for the Jesuits in the Roman Baroque style.
The church, with its barrel-vaulted single nave, side-chapels, transept and choir, has an imposing and elaborate interior: walls clad with green and white marble, massive pillars, colonnades, gilding and a High Altar with a baldachin and sculptured retable.
The most magnificent of the paintings is Titian's "Martyrdom of St Laurence" (between 1558 and 1560, last chapel on the left). Also noteworthy are Tintoretto's "Assumption of the Virgin" (in the left transept) and wall- and ceiling-paintings by Palma the Younger in the Sacristy.

Il Ghetto e Museo della Comunità Israelitica   G/H2
(Ghetto and Jewish Museum)

Location
Campo Ghetto Nuovo

Quay
Ferrovia

Opening times
Scuola Grande Tedesca
and Jewish Museum
Mon.–Fri. and Sun. 10 a.m.–
12.30 p.m.

Closed
Sat.

From 1090 Jews, who were not allowed into Venice itself, settled on the island of Spinalonga, later named Giudecca (see entry).
In 1395 the Jews quarrelled with the Christian population and had to leave Giudecca for Mestre.
In 1509, during the war against the League of Cambrai, they fled the flames of Mestre for the island city.
In 1516 the Senate allocated the site of a former iron-foundry, the Ghetto Nuovo, to the German and Italian Jews to live in. In 1541 the Jews arriving from the East were settled in the Ghetto Vecchio. The word "Ghetto" is said to be derived from "gettare" – to cast in metal – and this district was named after the foundries in it.

In 1633 this enclosed Jewish quarter was enlarged to include the Ghetto Nuovissimo (the "newest" ghetto).

The Jews were allowed only limited freedom of movement in the city, had to wear red or yellow hats and were not allowed to acquire land. The gates of the Ghetto remained locked from dusk until dawn. Infringements were punished by the Senate with large fines.

As decreed by the Senate, Jews were mostly dealers in second-hand goods and – subsequently – doctors.

Space was at a premium in the Ghetto so that houses as high as seven or eight storeys are not uncommon. The façades are plain, almost shabby.

It is, however, worth going inside the synagogues:

Guided tours of the synagogues three times each morning from the Museo della Comunità Israelitica

The Scuola Grande Tedesca (the Great German School) has been renovated and is now an intimate Baroque room with an oval gallery (an elegant way of compensating for the irregularity of the ground-plan) and some very fine individual pieces.

The Scuola Canton (Canton School) is the richly ornamented private house of prayer of the German-Jewish Canton family who made their fortune as bankers.

Another synagogue is the Scuola Italiana (Italian School).

The Scuola Levantina (Levantine School) is decorated with a pulpit by Andrea Brustolon (1662–1732).

The Scuola Spagnola (Spanish School) has a magnificent room created in the 17th c. by Baldassare Longhena, the most important exponent of the Venetian Baroque style (his best-known work is Santa Maria della Salute; see entry).

It is also worth paying a visit to the Museo della Comunità Israelitica (Museum of the Jewish Community).

Museo della Comunità Israelitica

This small but interesting museum, attached to the Scuola Grande Tedesca, contains objects used in worship, manuscripts and documents on the history of the Jews of Venice.

Giardinetto (Park)   K5/6

The Giardinetto, extending W of the Piazzetta (see entry) on the Molo, is one of those small parks which have grown up in Venice since the early 19th c. and which bring the touch of green to the city which many visitors find lacking.
Madame de Staël, for example, complained: "An indefinable sadness creeps into the heart when one arrives in Venice. One is not in the country, for there is no green tree to be seen and yet not in the town, for every sound is drowned out by the water."
It was to another French visitor (and the one most unwelcome to the city) that Venice owed her parks. Besides the Giardini Pubblici (see entry) Napoleon was also responsible for the Giardinetto behind the Procuratie Nuove (see entry) because

Location
Molo

Quay
San Marco

Church of Le Zitelle on the island of La Giudecca

he disliked having his view of the sea blocked by the grain store that stood there when he looked out of the window of the Procuratie Nuove.

Giardini Pubblici (public gardens)   O6, P6/7, Q7/8

Location
Riva dei Sette Martiri

Quay
Giardini

The Giardini Pubblici were laid out by Napoleon I at the SE end of the main island. Nowadays, however, much of the site is covered by the buildings which house the "Biennale", the biennial international art exhibition.

La Giudecca (island)   E–L7/8

Quay
Sant'Eufemia, Redentore,
Zitelle (Line 5 from
Riva degli Schiavoni,
Fondamenta delle Zattere)

The island of La Giudecca is thought to get its name from the Jews who lived here in the early Middle Ages. They were then moved to Mestre and subsequently ended up in the Ghetto (see entry).

The island is separated from the city by the broad Canal della Giudecca and divided into eight adjacent islands by small canals. Once a haven for Venetian nobles who had their villas here, today it is mostly inhabited by working-class families.

*Il Redentore (Church of the Redeemer)

Location
Campo Redentore

The Franciscan church is one of the main works of the Italian architect Andrea Palladio (1508–80). Much influenced by ancient Roman architecture, he based the façade of the Church of the Redeemer on three superimposed temple fronts.

The church and its festival both stem from 1576 when, to commemorate the end of the plague that year, the Senate vowed to build the church and to celebrate the Feast of the Redeemer; the religious services were entrusted to the Franciscans and the building of the church was begun in 1577 and completed in 1592.

Apart from Veronese's "The Baptism of Christ" and Alvise Vivarini's "Madonna in Adoration of the Child and two Angels" the church possesses no important paintings. After its consecration the Doge came here annually with the Signoria for the service of thanksgiving and the tradition is maintained to this day as every year the Venetians still make a pilgrimage to the church on the third Sunday in July, the Feast of the Redeemer, to give thanks for the ending of the epidemic. A bridge of boats is built from the Zattere over the Canal Giudecca which the procession crosses on its way to the Church of the Redeemer. The festival ends in the evening with magnificent firework displays and a parade of illuminated boats.

Quay
Redentore

Le Zitelle (officially: Santa Maria della Presentazione; church)

This church was planned by Andrea Palladio but built after his death. Although simpler and smaller than the Redentore it is still a fine building. It dates from the 16th c. but has no works of art of any significance.

Location
Fondamenta delle Zitelle

Quay
Zitelle

Libreria Vecchia di San Marco (Old Library)   K/L5

The Old Library on the W side of the Piazzetta opposite the Palazzo Ducale (see entries) is the masterpiece of Sansovino, the architect and sculptor, who worked on it between 1536 and 1553. After his death it was completed by Vincenzo Scamozzi to the original specifications.

The library, considered by Palladio the richest and most ornate building since antiquity, represents the real turning-point of Venetian architecture and the final break with Gothic Venice. Sansovino was a Florentine; he leaned towards the art of that region and towards Classical Rome. With this structure of Roman arcades, arches, columns, balustrades and sculptures Venice lost its own individual form of architecture, since from then on almost all new buildings, especially the palaces, were modelled on this particular innovation. This style of architecture also became known throughout Europe as a result of Scamozzi's theoretical work "Idea dell'architettura universale" (Idea of a universal architecture) which appeared in 1615.

The library itself is a unique work of art, elegant, harmonious and yet majestic.

The building (plan on page 60) today contains the exhibition rooms of the Biblioteca Nazionale Marciana, the "Library of St Mark". An impressive central portal (1533–54) by Alessandro Vittoria gives on to the staircase also with stuccoes also by Vittoria. The ceiling in the anteroom is adorned with "Fresco of Wisdom" by Titian (1560). The "Golden Hall" has 21 ceiling-medallions (three of them – "Geometry", "Arithmetic" and

Location
Piazzetta

Quay
San Marco

53

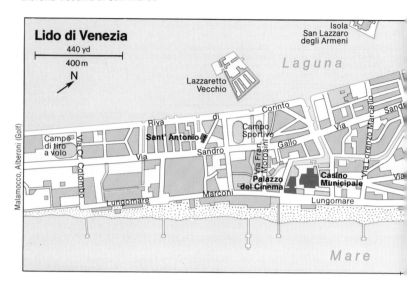

Part of the beach on the Lido

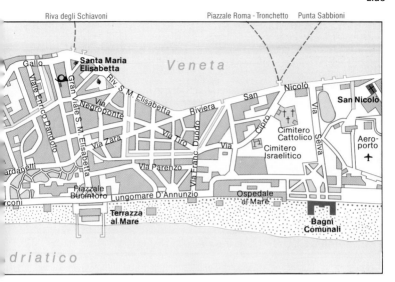

"Music" – by Veronese) and on the walls are 12 portraits of philosophers, five of them by Tintoretto.

The exhibition rooms contain an astonishing collection of gems, manuscripts, calligraphy and book illuminations, including the Grimani Breviary (1510–20) which alone has 831 pages of Flemish miniatures.

The actual Library of St Mark with its 750,000 volumes is today housed in the former Mint (Zecca, 1536), but is connected to the exhibition rooms.

Lido (island)

In previous centuries for Venetians the Lido only represented a trip into the country. Subsequently a fashionable resort, today it is a Mecca for tourists.

The island is 12 km (7½ miles) long, almost half of it a beach of fine smooth sand. Apart from the usual bathing (although each section of the beach belongs to one or several hotels there are two that are free), it has facilities for golf, tennis, horse-riding and clay-pigeon shooting as well as places of entertainment and a casino. In August and September every year the Lido is the venue for the International Film Festival (in the Palazzo del Cinema). The main architectural feature is its massive "fin de siècle" hotels (the hotel Des Bains and its beach was the setting for Thomas Mann's novel "Death in Venice"). In the N part of the island there are villas, functional modern buildings and hotels, beach and residential districts. Cars can be taken over by ferry; otherwise it is possible to get around on foot and by bus or cab or bicycle.

Quay
Santa Maria Elisabetta
(from Riva degli Schiavoni)

Car ferry
from Venice–Tronchetto

Loggetta di San Marco   K5

Location
Piazza di San Marco/
Campanile

Quay
San Marco

The Loggetta at the foot of the Campanile in the Piazza di San Marco (see entries), a small marble loggia built by Sansovino between 1537 and 1540, was originally intended for the members of the Great Council so that they could assemble here whenever they wished, sheltered from rain and snow, before going into the sessions.

However as early as 1569 the elegant building, a work of art in itself, was downgraded to being the guardroom of the Doges' Palace, which function it fulfilled until the end of the Republic in 1797.

In 1902 the Loggetta was crushed when the Campanile collapsed, but it was possible to rebuild it using the original stones and sculptures. Today it is a waiting-room for the tourists wanting to ascend the Campanile in the lift.

Sansovino's four bronze statues – "Pallas", "Apollo", "Mercury" and "Peace" – between the twin columns are masterpieces.

* Madonna dell'Orto (Santa Maria dell'Orto; church)   J2

Location
Fondamenta della Madonna
dell'Orto

Quay
San Marcuola

The charming brick façade of this church (dating from 1462), which represents a blend of Gothic and Renaissance, contains a large number of outstanding sculptures. Some of these are ascribed to Jacobello dalle Masegne, one of the sculptors influenced by the Late Gothic style of the N.

Madonna dell'Orto Church on the Rio della Madonna dell'Orto

In the interior is the tomb of Tintoretto, whose real name was Jacopo Robusti and who was buried in 1594 in the chapel to the right of the Presbytery (beside him lies his son Domenico). The church has several of his paintings: a "Last Judgment" (on the right of the choir), the "Worship of the Golden Calf" (on the left of the choir), "The Raising of Licinius by St Agnes" (fourth chapel on the left), the "Presentation of Mary in the Temple" (c. 1552) above the entrance to the Cappella di San Marco (in the right aisle).There are two noteworthy works by other artists: a "Madonna" (1480) by Giovanni Bellini (in the last chapel in the left aisle) and "St John the Baptist and four other Saints", a panel by Cima da Conegliano (1493; first altar on the right).

Church of St Mark

See Basilica di San Marco

Merceria (shopping street)   K4

The Merceria is Venice's main shopping street. It begins near the Rialto Bridge (see Ponte di Rialto) as a small square – in the centre is a statue commemorating the Italian dramatist Carlo Goldoni – and winds its way to St Mark's Square (see Piazza di San Marco), emerging under the clock tower (see Torre dell'Orologio). The shops in this famous street offer a cosmopolitan range of goods, the emphasis being on textiles, particularly lace, leather goods (shoes and handbags) and glassware from Murano. The many small cafés and restaurants ("rosticceria", "tavola calda") offer many delicacies and local specialities.
A feature of the Campo San Bartolomeo at the start of the Merceria, round the statue of Goldoni, is that this is still the place where businessmen meet to conduct their transactions.

Location
Merceria

Quay
Rialto/San Marco

** Monumento di Colleoni (Colleoni Monument)   L4

The monument to Colleoni is a brilliant piece of work from the Venetian Renaissance. The model was made by Andrea Verocchio (1481–88) but it was cast in bronze by Alessandro Leopardi in 1496. The splendour of the plinth, with its marble reliefs, is taken up by the vigour of the equestrian figure, so that one balances the other in complete harmony. The figure itself bears no resemblance to the real Bartolomeo Colleoni (1400–75) but is an evocation of what a "condottiere" should ideally look like – proud and conscious of his power.
Colleoni had commanded the land forces of the Republic, thus managing to amass a huge fortune. On his deathbed he bequeathed all his possessions to the State on the condition that a monument to his memory be erected "in front of San Marco". As the State (which hitherto had never authorised a public memorial) did not want to lose the money, instructions were given for the monument to be erected in front of the Scuola Grande di San Marco (see entry), the confraternity house of San Marco, that stands next to the Church of Santi

Location
Campo SS. Giovanni e Paolo

Quay
Rialto

Giovanni e Paolo (see Zanipolo), since the dying man had failed to specify that his monument must be in front of the "Church" of San Marco!

Municipio (Town Hall)   J/K5

Location
Campo San Luca

Quay
Rialto

The Town Hall consists of the Farsetti and Loredan palaces. Although the upper floors were altered in the 14th c., the ground floor of each palace has retained the 13th c. Byzantine floor plan.

---

*Murano (island)   N/O1 (A/B7/8)

Quay
Murano (Line 12 from
Fondamenta Nuove)

Opening times
Glasshouses:
weekdays

Once a pleasure park, where the rich nobility of Venice had their summer villas, the face of Murano was transformed when the Republic transferred the glass workshops here in 1291. Officially a safety measure to counteract the fire risk in central Venice, the unofficial reason, and probably the more likely one, was that this was the most effective method of safeguarding what until the 17th c. was Venice's best-kept secret, its method of glass-making. The glass-makers were well paid and enjoyed many privileges (they were allowed to carry swords and marry into the Venetian nobility) but were never allowed to leave the lagoon, thus retaining the knowledge of glass-making within Venice.

A Decree pf the Council of Ten of 1454 runs thus: "If a glass-blower takes his skill to another country to the detriment of the Republic he shall be ordered to return; should he refuse, his nearest relatives shall be thrown into prison so that his sense of family duty may induce him to return; should he persist in his disobedience secret measures shall be taken to eliminate him wherever he may be."

The art of the glass-blowers can be admired in the workshops; each factory has its own shop for the purchase of Murano glass – a rather expensive but characteristic souvenir!

The most important monument on the island is the Church of Santi Maria e Donato

Museo d'Arte Vetraria (Glass Museum)

Opening times
Mon., Tues., Thurs.–Sat.
10 a.m.–4 p.m., Sun. and
public holidays
9.30 a.m.–12.30 p.m

Closed
Wed.

Admission charge

The Glass Museum is housed in the Palazzo Giustinian which was built for the Bishop of Torcello in the 17th c. It contains one of the largest and most important collections of Venetian glass from the time of the Romans to the 20th c. – about 4,000 items. There are also displays of Bohemian and Moorish glass.

The most valuable piece is a 15th c. marriage bowl, dark blue and richly enamelled.

Most of the museum furnishings have been assembled from the churches on the island.

Santi Maria e Donato (church)

Location
Campo San Donato

This splendid church was built between the 7th and the 12th c. and combines Veneto-Byzantine and Early Romanesque features. Its façade with its superimposed arcades is justly famed.

Murano: glass-blowers

Murano: Glass Museum

Church of Santi Maria e Donato on Murano

The splendours of the interior include:
The columns of Greek marble with Veneto-Byzantine capitals which separate the two aisles from the nave, and the 12th c. mosaic floor with its animal figures.
The essential work of art is the mosaic of the Virgin (early 13th c.) over the apse.
The painted wooden panel with the figure of St Donato (above the first altar on the left) dated 1310, is the earliest example of Venetian painting. It is said that the Venetian Crusaders brought the body of St Donato to Venice from Euboea and gave it to the basilica, together with the remains of a dragon that Donato had killed; these relics can be seen on the wall behind the High Altar.
A Byzantine mosaic "Madonna at Prayer" (*c.* 1450).
Altar-piece with the death of the Virgin Mary on the wall of the left aisle (late 14th c.).
"The Madonna with Saints" in the entry to the Baptistery was painted by Lazzaro Bastiani in 1484.
A sarcophagus from Altinum in the Baptistery was once used as a font.

San Pietro Martire (church)

Location
Fondamenta Cavour

The 14th c. church (rebuilt in 1511 after a fire) contains several splendid Venetian paintings – Giovanni Bellini's "Madonna in Majesty with St Mark and the Doge Agostino Barbarigo" (1488; right aisle) and his "Assumption of the Virgin" which he painted between 1505 and 1513.
"St Jerome in the Wilderness" and "St Agatha in Prison" (left aisle) are by Paolo Veronese.

Museo Archeologico (Archaeological Museum)   K/L5

Location
Piazzetta

Only some of the museum's exhibits are in fact archaeological treasures but the museum offers a unique opportunity

Museo Archeologico

A Entrance to the Museum
B Entrance to the Library

Vestibolo
Piazzetta
Libreria Vecchia di San Marco
Libreria Sansoviniana

Courtyard
Entrance
Courtyard

Offices
Curator's office

Piazza San Marco

FIRST FLOOR (PRIMO PIANO)
1 Corridor: Greek inscriptions
2 Coins
3 Copies of Greek sculptures
4 Greek sculptures
5 Roman copies of Greek sculptures
6 Dionysos and satyr; Grimani Altar, etc.
7 Hellenistic objets d'art
8 Galatian figures; Odysseus, etc.
9–10 Mainly Roman busts
11 Roman reliefs; Byzantine ivory-carvings
12–13 Roman art
14 Corridor: Roman art
15 Roman inscriptions
16 Unknown copies
17 Religious reliefs, etc.
18 Sculptures, statuettes, etc.
19 Objets d'art (ceramics, bronzes)
20 Assyrian reliefs; Egyptian mummies

to compare Classical archaeological finds with "modern"
Renaissance art. Here the visitor can see the Classical
sculptures that influenced the Renaissance artists of Venice.

The most important exhibits:
Room 4: eleven Classical Greek korai dressed in chitons
(5th c. B.C.).
Room 5: Statue of Apollo.
Room 6: Satyr and nymph embracing.
Room 7: Carved gem-stones.
Room 8: Running Odysseus (Hellenistic); Leda and the Swan;
Roman busts.
Rooms 9–10: Busts from the Republic and Roman Empire.
Room 11: Byzantine ivory-carvings; St John the Evangelist and
St Paul (10th c.); St Theodore and St George.
Room 12: Reliefs of centaurs by T. Aspetti.
Room 20: Assyrian reliefs (8th–7th c. B.C.).

Quay
San Marco

Opening times
Tues.–Sat. 9 a.m.–2 p.m.;
Sun. and public holidays
9 a.m.–1 p.m.

Museo della Comunità Israelitica (Jewish Museum)

See Il Ghetto

Quay
Ferrovia

* Museo Civico Correr e Museo del Risorgimento   K5
(Correr Museum and Risorgimento Museum)

The Correr Museum consists of an interesting collection
illustrating the history of Venice and an important collection of
paintings. The main section covers both floors of the Procuratie
and the entrance is in the passage in the Ala Napoleonica (see
entries).
The first floor is devoted to the historical collections – (Rooms
1–14): documents, etc. illustrating the architectural development of the city (Room 1); paintings of scenes from the history
of Venice; documents on the development of the State coat of
arms, on the history of the Doges and the political institutions;
(Rooms 3–10): State robes of Doges, Procurators and
Senators, a large collection of Venetian coins; finally,
documents, etc. illustrating the history of Venetian shipping.
The second floor houses an art gallery with paintings from the
14th to the 17th c., including works by Lorenzo Veneziano,
Jacobello del Fiore, Cosmè Tura, Antonello da Messina, the
Bellini brothers, Alvise Vivarini and Carpaccio, including the
last-named's famous *Courtesans*.
The Flemish masters are represented by Hugo van der Goes,
Dirk Bouts, Rogier van der Weiden and Pieter Brueghel.

Location
Procuratie Nuove
Piazza di San Marco
(entrance: Ala Napoleonica)

Quay
San Marco

Opening times
Mon., Wed.–Sat. 10 a.m.–
4 p.m.; Sun. and public
holidays 9 a.m.–12.30 p.m.

Closed
Tues.

Admission charge

Museo del Risorgimento

The Museo del Risorgimento contains documents and
illustrations of Venice's struggle against Austria, the 1848
Revolution led by Daniele Manin and union with the Kingdom
of Sardinia-Piedmont in 1866.

Museo di Icone dell'Istituto Ellenico (Icon Museum)   M5

Location
Salizzada dei Greci

Quay
San Zaccaria

The former Scuola di San Niccolò dei Greci (Palazzo Flangini), to the left of the Church of San Giorgio dei Greci, houses a small but interesting icon museum. Apart from 14th–18th c. icons it also contains sumptuous richly embroidered liturgical robes and a collection of liturgical objects.
The Palazzo Flangini was built by Longhena in the 17th c.
Opening times: Mon.–Fri. 9.30 a.m.–12.30 p.m., 3.30–5 p.m.; Sun. 9–noon. Admission charge.

Museo Marciano (Museum of San Marco)

See Basilica di San Marco, Museo Marciano

Museo dell'Opera di Palazzo

See Palazzo Ducale

Museo di Storia Naturale

See Fondaco dei Turchi

Museo Storico Navale (Museum of Naval History)   N6

Location
Riva San Biagio

Quay
Arsenale

The Museum of Naval History uses models, mementoes and documents to give an account of shipbuilding and the types of vessels afloat in the period that Venice was a sea power, ending in 1797.
There is a model of the legendary ship of state, "Bucintoro", also on display here. The Doge's sumptuous State galley was burnt out during the 1798 Jacobin Revolution.
Opening times: Tues.–Sat. 9 a.m.–1.30 p.m., Sun. and public holidays 9 a.m.–noon. Closed Mon. Admission charge.

Napoleonic Wing

See Ala Napoleonica

* Palazzo dei Camerlenghi (Palace of the Lords of the Exchequer)   K4

Location
Campo San Giacomo/
Ponte di Rialto
(entrance)

Quay
Rialto

With its attractive mezzo-reliefs and harmonious proportions, this prettily impressive white marble building on the Rialto was built in 1525–28 by Guglielmo Grigi and was once the seat of the three Lords of the Venetian Exchequer. Its best side can be seen either from the Canal Grande or from the Ponte di Rialto (see entry).

* Palazzo Contarini del Bovolo   J5

The Palazzo Contarini del Bovolo is probably the only palace in
Venice which has a courtyard that is more interesting than the
façade overlooking the Canal (in this case the Rio dei
Barcaroli). In the courtyard is the famous Scala di Bovolo, a
spiral staircase built about 1500 by the architect Giovanni
Candi, which gave the palace its nickname ("bovolo"=spiral).

Location
Calle della Vida/
Rio dei Barcaroli

Quay
Rialto

* Palazzo Corner della Ca' Grande   H/J6

The palace is one of the finest examples of High Renaissance
architecture and today is the seat of the Prefettura (Prefecture).
This huge palace (hence its name: "Ca' Grande"=big house)
was built in the 16th c. by Jacopo Sansovino, the Italian
master-builder and sculptor, for the Cornaro family.
He gave the façade (overlooking the Canal Grande) Ionic
columns on the first floor and Corinthian columns on the
second.
The interior was restored and modified in the 19th c. The main
façade overlooks the Canal Grande.

Location
Canal Grande/
Fondamenta Corner Zaguri
(entrance)

Quay
Santa Maria del Giglio

* Palazzo Corner della Regina   J3/4

The outstanding feature of this huge Baroque palace, built in
1724 by Domenico Rossi, is the frieze of grotesque heads in the
façade just above the water-level.
The building was converted (unfortunately) from the Palazzo
of Caterina Corner, Queen of Cyprus. The Corners, an old-
established Venetian noble family, became so rich and
powerful as a result of their sugar-cane plantations on Cyprus
that the King of the island, James II, married the 18-year-old
Caterina Corner in 1472. Eight months later the King died of
poisoning. Caterina was forced to cede her kingdom to the
Republic of Venice and in return was given Asolo as domain in
exile and was allowed to spend the rest of her life (d. 1510) in
her palace on the Canal Grande in a manner befitting her
station. This is how Venice acquired Cyprus.
Queen Caterina's palace today houses Venice's pawnshop.
The main façade overlooks the Canal Grande.

Location
Calle Regina

Quay
San Staè

* Palazzo Corner-Spinelli   H5

Designed by Mauro Coducci in 1490–1510 besides the twin-
arched windows and the curved balconies, the particularly
remarkable feature of this palace is its upper storey with its rich
yet well-ordered ornamentation.
The interior was designed in 1542 by Sanmicheli.
The main façade overlooks the Canal Grande.

Location
Rio Ca' Corner/
Canal Grande

Quay
Sant'Angelo

*Palazzo Dolfin-Manin   K4

Location
Riva del Ferro/Canal Grande

Quay
Rialto

This huge palace with its impressive façade was built between 1538 and 1560 by Sansovino. It was the residence of the 120th and last Doge, Ludovico Manin, during his time in office (1789–97). Today it houses the Banca d'Italia.

Manin's election to the office of Doge, when he declared himself in such a state of trepidation that he hardly knew what he was doing, was followed, on 12 May 1797, with his being obliged to declare the dissolution of the 1,000-year-old Republic of St Mark when, with the words "It will not be needed any more" he handed over his insignia of office. He had to make his country residence, Campo Formio in Friuli, available for the negotiations that led to Napoleon's handing the city on the water over to Austria as a "consolation prize".

Palazzo Ducale (Doges' Palace)   L5

Location
Piazzetta

Quay
Riva degli Schiavoni

Opening times
8.30 a.m.–6 p.m. daily

Admission charge

The Doges' Palace was the centre of government of the Republic and the residence of the Doge (see General Information, Government of the Venetian City State under the Doges). Apparently a square building, it actually consists of only three wings: the wing along the Rio Palazzo, the main façade on the Molo (71 m (233 ft)) and the W façade (75 m (246 ft)) overlooking the Piazzetta. The fourth wing is formed by the Basilica di San Marco (Basilica of St Mark, see entry) which the palace has adjoined since 1438.

The first palace of the Doges, a wretched gloomy wooden fortress with massive defensive towers, was built in 814. It was surrounded by the lagoon on the S and canals on the other sides. This castle was entered by a drawbridge on the N side. After frequent destruction by fire and subsequent rebuilding, the castle was converted in the 12th c. into a palace in the Byzantine style. Fragments of the foundations are all that remain of these early Palazzi.

The present palace was built mainly in the 14th c., and the façade overlooking the Piazzetta mostly dates from the first half of the 15th c.

The courtyard and the main interior were reconstructed in the Renaissance style after a fire in 1483. The first architect was Filippo Calendario; the master-builders of the Bon family used his plans to complete the two main façades in the Gothic-Venetian style in the years leading up to 1462. The palace was completed in 1550. The palace survived two further fires – one in 1574 and another in 1577.

Exterior

The astonishing exterior of the palace is often referred to as a symbol of the "city on piles". The fragile filigree of the Loggia with its 71 columns and almost Oriental tracery stands on the 36 short columns of the ground floor. Above is a huge block of marble with six large windows and a richly ornamented Gothic balcony. It is faced with white and pink marble in a diamond pattern. On top is a cornice of merlons and spires. The amazing tension created by this combination caused André Suarès to exclaim: "So much graceful strength on such fragile foundations!"

Façade of the Palazzo Ducale

S front
The S façade with its two lower Gothic windows is the oldest part of the exterior. The beautiful capitals symbolising Vice and Virtue (14th–15th c.) are worthy of note. The large balcony window dates from 1404; the figure on the gable, Venice as "Justice", was dated in 1579.

W front
The W façade is mostly 15th c. It copies the style of the S front (balcony windows, gable statue). The capitals here (allegorical themes, foliage) are also noteworthy.
In earlier times sentences of death used to be proclaimed from a position between the ninth and tenth columns of the Loggia (easy to spot as they are the only ones made of red marble).

Porta della Carta
The Porta della Carta (the main entrance) was created as the link between the Doges' Palace and the Basilica by the brothers Giovanni and Bartolomeo Bon (1438–42). Together with the Ca' d'Oro (see entry) it is considered a perfect example of Venetian Gothic.
The door is surrounded by a framework of ornamentation and allegorical figures; above is Doge Francesco Foscari kneeling before the Lion of St Mark (symbolising the attitude of the Venetians towards their State: the individual bows to the power of the State; see General Information, Government of the Venetian City State under the Doges). The present sculpture is a 19th c. copy of the original which was destroyed in 1797.
The Porta della Carta (Paper Gate) is thought to be so named from the petitioners who used to wait here for the members of

the Council and the Government in order to hand over their petitions and requests. The laws of the Republic were also proclaimed in front of the gate, at the corner of the Basilica di San Marco, on the stump of a column used for that purpose.

Foscari Arch
The Porta della Carta leads into the courtyard through the Foscari Arch, a Gothic porch richly ornamented with columns, niches and turrets and already displaying elements of the Renaissance style, especially in the statues of Adam and Eve by the sculptor Antonio Rizzo (these are copies, the originals stand in the Quarantia Criminal on the second floor).

Courtyard
The courtyard, redesigned by Antonio Rizzo after a fire in 1483, is a Renaissance masterpiece. After Rizzo fled (he had been accused of embezzlement) the upper part of the main façade of the courtyard was completed by his successors; the W and S façades were refaced at the beginning of the 17th c.

The richly ornamented well-heads (16th c.) are especially noteworthy.

Cortile dei Senatori
Left of the main courtyard is the Cortile dei Senatori with a Late Renaissance front and beautiful marble ornamentation. This is where the Senators used to gather before receptions. The little chapel next to it was the Doge's private chapel (now closed).

Scala dei Giganti
The Staircase of the Giants, also designed and begun by Rizzo, adjoins the Foscari Arch and leads up to the State apartments on the first floor. Its top landing is where the Doges were crowned (and, in the case of Doge Marino Faliero, beheaded). The Coronation procedure was for the newly elected Doge to take his oath, whereupon the youngest member of the Great Council would hand him the white "corno" (Doge's cap) and the senior member would place it on his head.

The staircase owes its name to the two larger-than-life-size figures of Mars and Neptune symbolising Venice's power on land and sea. They are the work of Jacopo Sansovino (1567).

Interior of the Palace

The Palazzo Ducale is now a museum but, unlike the general run of museums, the paintings on display here were created especially to decorate the Doges' Palace, not added later. Together with the sumptuous setting – stucco-work, gilding, decorated walls and ceilings – they are a reflection of all the magnificence displayed by the Republic of Venice. Visitors follow a marked itinerary.

Scala d'Oro
The main and side staircases of the Scala d'Oro lead from the Loggia on the first floor to the second floor and thence to the offices and reception rooms on the third floor. In earlier times only members of the Council and the Doge's guests of honour were allowed to use them.

This impressive staircase, which gets its name from its rich gold ornamentation, was probably begun by Sansovino in 1538 and completed by Scarpagnino about 1550.

Scala dei Giganti: the Giants' Staircase, designed by Rizzo

Sala del Senato in the Palazzo Ducale

Atrio Quadrato

This anteroom contains a remarkable ceiling-painting by Tintoretto of the Doge Girolamo Priuli (1561–64) appearing before Venice and with Justice presenting him with the Sword and the Scales in the presence of his Patron Saint and Peace. All the wall-paintings are also based on the theme of Venice.

Sala delle Quattro Porte

The Hall of the Four Doors was decorated in accordance with Palladio's designs. The ceiling and the frescoes are from the Studio of Tintoretto. The wall-painting "Doge Antonio Grimani before the Faith" was begun by Titian about 1600 and completed by another artist.

Sala dell'Anticollegio

This beautiful, richly decorated hall was mainly used as a waiting-room for foreign delegations. The paintings are by Tintoretto, Paolo Veronese and Jacopo Bassano.

Tintoretto's four paintings are based on mythological events and give a new interpretation to the history of Venice: "Minerva dismissing Mars" (victory of wisdom over force); "Vulcan and Cyclops forging weapons for Venice"; "Mercury and the Three Graces" (Venice's commercial activities are recompensed by beauty); "The Marriage of Bacchus and Ariadne" (Venice's marriage with the sea).

Napoleon had Veronese's "Rape of Europa" taken to Paris. It was later returned together with other art treasures.

Bassano's painting depicts the scene from the Old Testament of the return of Jacob with his family.

Sala del Collegio

This hall, probably the most beautiful room in the whole palace, is where the "Collegio" (the Cabinet of the Government) met under the Chairmanship of the Doge and where the Republic received its most important visitors. (See the Government of the Venetian City State under the Doges, Collegio.)

What most impresses the visitor are the harmonious proportions of the room and the unity of decorations and furnishings. The large wall-painting of 1578 above the Doge's throne is by Veronese and depicts Doge Sebastiano Venici offering thanks to Christ for the victory of the Venetians over the Turks in the Battle of Lepanto.

The ceiling by Francesco Bello is the finest in the palace and has a wonderful series of paintings by Veronese (*c.* 1577). As everywhere else in the palace, these paintings take as their subjects the ideals that formed the basis of the State of Venice: "Mars and Neptune" (power on land and sea), "Faith" (piety), "Justice and Peace". The borders depict the virtues of the State: dog (fidelity), horn of plenty (industry), crane (vigilance), spider's web (diligence), eagle (self-control), sceptre (magnanimity), dove (peaceableness), lamb (meekness).

The wall-paintings are by Tintoretto or his pupils. Near the entrance is Tintoretto's "Doge Andrea Gritti kneeling before the Virgin".

Sala del Senato

The Senate met twice a week in this hall. Consisting of the Doge, members of the College and some 60 members of the Great Council, the Senate laid down policy guidelines and made decisions on peace and war.

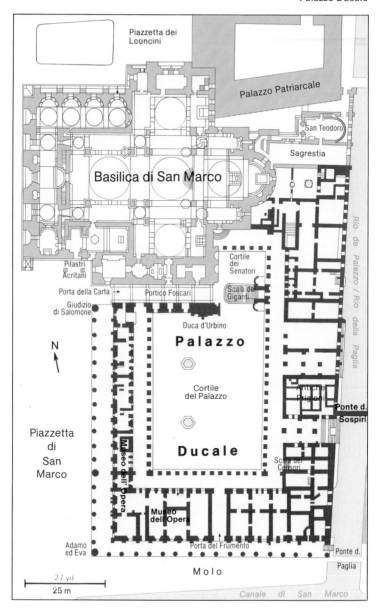

Most of the paintings are by Jacopo Palma the Younger and reiterate the theme of the glorification of Venice.

Private chapel (not always accessible)
The Doge's private chapel has a fine "Madonna" by Sansovino.

Sala del Consiglio dei Dieci
The Council of Ten, which sat here, was the secret State court. It was in charge of the secret police and controlled every aspect of public and private life. There was no appeal against a judgment given by the Ten.
A harmonious blend of wood panelling, gilding and paintings, this room's works of special interest are the ceiling-paintings, including Veronese's "Jupiter hurling his thunderbolts against the Vices", a copy of the original in the Louvre and an allusion to the work of the Council of Ten and "Juno offering the Ducal Crown to Venice".

Sala della Bussola
The wooden compass in the right-hand corner gave this room its name (there are two doors hidden behind it). In this room those summoned to appear before the Council of Ten waited to be examined. Next to the door is a Bocca di Leone ("lion's mouth"), into which secret denunciations could be dropped (see General Information, Government of the Venetian City State under the Doges).

Sala dei Tre Capi
This room belonged to the three Chief Magistrates elected from the Council of Ten to form the Court of Inquisition which dealt with acts of high treason and espionage and kept the nobles under surveillance. Anyone brought before them was as good as dead.

Sala dei Inquisitori
The inquisitors, who met here, were the examining magistrates whose task was to interrogate offenders, if necessary with the aid of red-hot pincers, the rack and the thumbscrew.
The room was originally covered entirely in leather. The picture in the middle of the ceiling is Tintoretto's "Return of the Prodigal Son".

Armoury
The next rooms once housed the armoury of the Republic and nowadays have over 2,200 weapons and suits of armour (mostly 15th–16th c.) on display.

Andito del Maggior Consiglio
This "vestibule" with its gilded ceiling beams is where the members of the Great Council waited before the sessions and during the breaks.

Sala della Quarantia Civil Vecchia
The civil court that sat here consisted of a body of 40 (hence Quarantia) lawyers.
The framed picture of the Virgin dates from the 15th c. and the large wall-paintings from the 17th c.

Sala del Guariento
This room contains the undamaged fragments of the large

fresco painted in 1365 by the artist Guariento (hence the room's name) for the Sala del Maggior Consiglio (Hall of the Great Council) which was burnt out by the great fire of 1577.

Sala del Maggior Consiglio
This Hall of the Great Council, the seat of the Lower House of the Venetian Parliament, is impressive not so much because of its size (54 × 25 m (177 × 82 ft)) but because of its harmonious proportions in relation to its size. It was made so large not simply in order to be imposing but also on purely practical grounds since when the Council was in session it had to accommodate up to 1,800 citizens entitled to vote. It, therefore, had rows of seats in the middle, along the two long walls and against the W wall; the short E wall with the tribune was reserved for the Doge and the highest officials. The hall was built between 1340 and 1355.
The greatest artists of their time took part in painting the room. From Padua came Guariento, whose painting above the Doge's throne was destroyed by fire (see Sala del Guariento) and replaced in 1588 by Tintoretto's "Paradise" which is still in place. The fire of 1577 also destroyed the paintings by Gentile da Fabriano, Pisanello, Giovanni Bellini, Carpaccio and Titian. Reconstruction (in its original form) was entrusted to Antonio da Ponte, who built the Ponte di Rialto (see entry). Tintoretto and Veronese did the paintings, assisted by Palma the Younger and Francesco Bassano.
Tintoretto's "Paradise" (22 × 7 m (71 × 23 ft)) ranks as the largest oil-painting in the world and its great swarm of figures makes it difficult for the viewer to take in the picture as a whole. Closer inspection shows that Tintoretto ranged the figures in accordance with their rank, based on the order of the litany, grouping them in circles and segments of circles with Christ and his Mother in the centre at the top.

Another masterpiece is the ceiling with panels painted by Veronese – "Venezia", Venice surrounded by gods and crowned by Victory.
Tintoretto's other masterly ceiling-paintings are "Doge Ponte paying homage to Venice" and Palma the Younger's "Venice welcoming the conquered Nations around her Throne".
The wall canvases depict scenes from Venetian history. The frieze, just under the ceiling, of the first 76 Doges is the work of Domenico Tintoretto and his assistants; the portrait of Doge Marino Faliero, who was beheaded, has been painted out in black (see General Information, Government of the Venetian City State).
The Sala del Maggior Consiglio was where all the decisions that made the Republic a World Power were discussed. It was also where the Republic was declared to have been dissolved in 1797.

The tour now takes the visitor to the Doge's apartments on the second floor of the E wing.

Sala dello Scrutinio
The Voting Hall was where public elections, including the election of the Doge, were prepared and carried out. The paintings, including Tintoretto's "The Conquest of Zara" (right wall) depict Venetian battles on land and sea.

Palazzo Ducale

Magnificent oriel window in the Palazzo Ducale

Ponte dei Sospiri

Sala dello Scudo
The maps, copies of originals of about 1540, document Venetian rule.

Sala Grimani
Special features are the ceiling, with its gold ornamentation on a blue ground, and the frieze of allegorical subjects (after 1504).

Sala Erizzo
An interesting 16th c. ceiling and 15th–17th c. marble and stucco chimneypiece.

Sala degli Stucchi
The stucco on the vaulted ceiling dates from the 17th c.; the stucco and painted inserts on the walls were added in the 18th c.

Small staircase of the Doges
Above the door is a fresco by Titian, "St Christopher" (1523–24), the only painting by Titian in the Doges' Palace to have survived.

Sala dei Filosofi
This vestibule gave access to the Doge's apartments.

Pinacoteca
The rooms at the back of the Doge's apartments contain a small picture gallery with works by Giovanni Bellini, Hieronymus Bosch, Boccaccio Boccaccini, Antonello de Saliba, Tiepolo and Tintoretto.

Ponte dei Sospiri
The Bridge of Sighs is an enclosed arched bridge over the Rio di Palazzo joining the first floor of the Doge's Palace with the first floor of the prison.
Completed by Antonio da Ponte in 1603, today it is one of Venice's main tourist attractions, though less because of its attractive Baroque shape than because of its name and significance; it was over this bridge that prisoners were taken before the judges, and the sentences given by Venetian judges were as hard and unmerciful as the laws of the Republic.

Prigioni
Until about 1750 there were no escapes from the State prison and even Casanova only managed to get out by an extremely hazardous route.
Especially feared were the piombi "lead chambers", the low narrow cells right under the lead roof which were like furnaces in summer.
The cells once had wooden walls, ceilings and floors but now only the stone walls and iron-barred windows are left.

*Palazzo Grassi   H5

The Palazzo Grassi was built in the second half of the 18th century by the architect Giorgio Massari for the Grassi family, who lived there until the beginning of the 20th century.
The three-storeyed building with its relatively plain façade was completely restored internally in 1984/5 and partly rebuilt. It is reported that the Palazzo Grassi will become a "great European cultural centre" and that it will be the venue for a comprehensive summer exhibition and a smaller winter one.

Location
Canal Grande

Quay
Campo San Samuele

*Palazzo Grimani   J5

The palace was built in 1556, where the Rio di San Luca flows into the Canal Grande, for the Procurator Girolamo Grimani by Michele Sanmicheli who came from Verona. The towering façade with its massive window arches was completed by Giangiacomo dei Grigi the following year. The solid-looking palace is usually considered very un-Venetian.
Today it houses the Appeal Court of Venice.
The main façade overlooks the Canal Grande.

Location
Canal Grande/Rio di San Luca

Quay
Rialto

*Palazzo Loredan dell'Ambasciatore   G6

A marvellous Gothic palace; on the façade are two especially interesting sea-horses, by a follower of Vittoria.
In the 18th c. the palace was the residence of the Ambassador of the Holy Roman Empire, hence its popular name "Palazzo del Ambasciatore" (Ambassador's Palace).
The main façade overlooks the Canal Grande.

Location
Calle dei Cerchieri

Quay
Ca' Rezzonico

Magnificent façade of the Palazzo Pesaro

*Palazzo Pesaro, Galleria d'Arte Moderna e Galleria d'Arte Orientale

J3

Location
Fondamenta Mocenigo/
Canal Grande

Quay
San Staè

Opening times
Closed for restoration

The palace was built between 1652 and 1710 by the masters of Venetian Late Baroque, Baldassare Longhena and Antonio Gaspari. Sansovino's Library (see Libreria Vecchia) in the Piazzetta (see entry) was used as a model for the splendid façade.

Today the lavishly designed interior houses the Galleria d'Arte Moderna (Gallery of Modern Art). The gallery was founded at the end of the last century and has one of the most important collections of modern art in Italy. Among its most interesting exhibits are works by the Munich Realist Franz von Lenbach, the Munich Secessionist Franz von Stuck, Auguste Rodin, Marc Chagall and Klimt.

On the third floor is the Museo d'Arte Orientale (Museum of Oriental Art). It has an outstanding collection of Far Eastern objets d'art, e.g. Chinese vases, Japanese paintings, Indian sculpture.

The main façade overlooks the Canal Grande.

Palazzo Querini-Stampalia (library and museum)

L5

Location
Campiello Querini-Stampalia

The attractive palace houses the Querini-Stampalia art gallery and library which were bequeathed to the city, together with the palace, in 1868.

Palazzo Rezzonico on the Canal Grande

The art gallery is open from Tuesday till Saturday from 10 a.m. to 4 p.m. and on Sundays and public holidays from 10 a.m. until 3 p.m.

Quay
Rialto

Admission charge

Biblioteca Querini-Stampalia
The library is on the first floor. It has over 120,000 Venetian volumes and manuscripts.

Pinacoteca Querini-Stampalia
The collection of 14th–18th c. Venetian paintings is on the second floor. The pictures are still arranged according to the wishes of the founder of the collection Count Giovanni Querini-Stampalia. There are works by Gabriel Bella (Room 1), Donato Veneziano (Room 2), Sebastiano Bombelli, Marco Vecellio (Room 3), Palma the Younger, Luca Giordano (Room 4), Andrea Schiavone (Room 5), Pietro Liberi, Matteo dei Pitocchi (Rooms 6–7), Giovanni Bellini, Lorenzo di Credi (Room 8), Palma the Elder (Room 9), Pietro Longhi (Rooms 11–13), Alessandro Longhi, Giambattista Tiepolo (Room 18), and Bernardo Strozzi (Room 19).
Apart from paintings the Venetian 18th c. furniture is of special interest.

*Palazzo Rezzonico e Museo del Settecento Veneziano   G5
(Museum of 18th c. Venice)

The massive building was begun in 1667 by Venice's greatest Baroque architect, Baldassare Longhena, and completed nearly 100 years later (1752) by Giorgio Massari for the noble

Location
Rio di Santa Barnabà/
Canal Grande

Quay
Ca' Rezzonico

Rezzonico family. One member of this family, who in 1687 had bought himself the Venetian patent of nobility, as Pope Clement XIII.

Museo del Settecento Veneziano

Opening times
Mon.–Thurs., Sat. 10 a.m.–
4 p.m., Sun. 9 a.m.–
12.30 p.m.

Closed
Fri.

Admission charge

The museum's collection, in keeping with the design and decoration of the palace, gives a fascinating glimpse of life in Venice in the Rococo period. There are some 40 display rooms: silk wall-coverings, Flemish tapestries, cabinets and chests of drawers (including some splendid pieces by Andrea Brustolon), the Chinoiserie and lacquered furniture so popular at that time, Venetian porcelain and pottery, bronzes and puppets. Of especial interest are the original 18th c. Venetian costumes and a meticulously reconstructed 18th c. chemist's shop and theatre (third floor).

The palace contains several celebrated ceiling-paintings by G. B. Tiepolo including "The Allegory of Marriage" (that between Ludovico Rezzonico and Faustina Savorgnan) in Room 2; "Merit, between Nobility and Virtue" in the Throne Room, and "Strength and Wisdom" in Room 6.

*Palazzo Vendramin-Calergi   H3

Location
Calle Colombia/
Canal Grande

Quay
San Marcuola

This palace is a perfect example of Venetian Renaissance architecture and towards the end of the last century many of its elements were copied throughout Europe.

The palace as built between 1480 and 1504 by Mauro Coducci. At first it belonged to the Loredan family, then in the 16th c. to the Calergi family, and finally in the 18th c. it came into the hands of the Vendramin family. Richard Wagner died here in 1883.

In winter it houses Venice's casino.

Pescheria (fish market)   J4

Location
Canal Grande/Ponte di
Rialto (access)

Although only dating from 1907 (yet surprisingly unobtrusive) the market hall with its skilful architecture (especially the ingenious capitals on the columns) serves its purpose well. It was constructed on over 18,000 piles of larchwood completely in accordance with the centuries-old method.

**Piazza di San Marco (St Mark's Square)   K5

Quay
San Marco

St Mark's Square, "la Piazza" for short, is Venice on parade, the point round which Venetian life revolves. Considered one of the finest squares in the world, it conveys a perfect impression of the city's former greatness since round it are grouped the buildings on which were centred the civic and religious life of the Republic. Surrounded on three sides by the arcades of public buildings – the Procuratie Vecchie (N), the Ala Napoleonica (W) and the Procuratie Nuove (S) – the integrated beauty of this unique square is rounded off by the

Piazzetta di San Marco looking towards the Basilica

domes and arches of the Basilica di San Marco (E) and the slender, soaring Campanile (see entries).

The square, paved with trachyte, is completely open without a single monument or roadway to detract from the unbroken architectural unity. The only traffic is the visitors (and the famous pigeons).

The square becomes narrower as it approaches the Ala Napoleonica, which gives it considerably greater depth: over an average length of 175 m (574 ft) it narrows from a width of 82 m (269 ft) at the Basilica to 56·6 m (185·6 ft) at the other end.

Originally the Piazza was full of fruit trees with a canal running across it. The completion of the Basilica and the enlargement of the Palazzo Ducale (Doges' Palace; see entry) also saw a start made on landscaping the square. First came the Campanile (begun in 912 and completed in the 12th c.; it suddenly collapsed on 14 July 1902 when an exact reproduction was built and opened on 25 April 1912), followed in 1204 by the Procuratie Vecchie (reconstructed in 1512 after a fire); the fruit trees disappeared, the canal was filled in and in 1267 the square covered with paving-slabs; 1582 saw the building of the Procuratie Nuove. Having been paved with marble in 1735 (the big white squares originally marked the sites where the individual craftsmen's guilds were allowed to erect their market-stalls), the square finally acquired its present aspect with the building of the Napoleonic Wing.

Until the fall of the Republic the Piazza di San Marco was a "market-place". Today it is a place to see and be seen, to stroll or sit and listen to the bands performing at the square's world-famous cafés.

The pigeons of San Marco are also part of the picture. Fed at the

St Theodore on his column in the Piazzetta

Ponte di Rialto

public charge (although there are no set feeding-times), they are the acknowledged protégés of the Venetians. Whatever their origins – whether descended from the birds brought to the lagoon in the 5th c. by the early Venetians on their flight from Attila, or from those set free by the Doges each Palm Sunday, or even from the carrier pigeons that brought the news of the capture of Constantinople in 1204 – they are an institution.

Piazzetta   K/L5

This charming square is where Venice really receives its visitors – open to the sea, with the two columns on the Molo (Colonne di Marco e Teodoro), bordered on the right by the Palazzo Ducale (Doges' Palace), on the left by the Libreria Vecchia (library), backed by the Campanile on one side and the projecting Basilica di San Marco (Basilica of St Mark) on the other with, in the background, the Torre dell'Orologio (Clock Tower) and the Procuratie (see entries).

Quay
San Marco

The Piazzetta opens into the Piazza di San Marco (see entry) and is almost a part of it.

It acquired its present shape with the building of the library. In the early Middle Ages a broad canal ran alongside the Doge's Palace up to the Basilica di San Marco.

Ponte dell'Accademia (Academy Bridge)   H6

For centuries the only bridge over the Canal Grande was the Ponte di Rialto (see entry), then in 1854 Austria, the occupying Power since 1815 when Venice became part of the Habsburg Kingdom of Lombardy-Veneto, decided to erect a second foot-bridge and the Ponte dell'Accademia, a small iron bridge, was built. In 1932 the iron bridge was demolished and replaced by a wooden bridge. Looked upon as a stopgap, it was to be replaced by a stone bridge, but the stone bridge was never built. At present the Ponte dell'Accademia is not accessible because it is unsafe.

Quay
Accademia

*Ponte di Rialto (Rialto Bridge)   K4

For a long time the Ponte di Rialto was the only foot-bridge over the Canal Grande (the Ponte dell'Accademia (see entry) was not built until 1854 and the Ponte Scalzi near the station is 20th c.). It gets its name from "Rivus Altus" (high bank), which was what the earliest settlement on the island was first called.

Location
Ponte di Rialto

Quay
Rialto

The first wooden bridge was built on this spot as early as 1180, later to be replaced by a drawbridge which collapsed in 1444 under the weight of a crowd of people who had gathered to watch a boat procession.

Almost 150 years later, in 1588, the Venetians embarked upon the venture of building a stone bridge. Designed by Antonio de Ponte, the bridge is supported by 6,000 piles on each side and its single arch is 22 m (72 ft) in span and 7·5 m (24 ft) high.

Procuratie Vecchie in the Piazza di San Marco

Procuratie (Procurators' Offices)   K5

Location
Piazza di San Marco

Quay
San Marco

The N and S sides of the Piazza di San Marco (see entry) are bordered by the Procuratie, the former offices of the Procurators of San Marco, the chief officials of the Republic. Today they house, "inter alia", the Museo Correr, together with the Museo del Risorgimento, and the Museo Archeologico (see entries).

There was a "Procurator" as early as the 10th c. After the Doge he was the most important man in the State and was answerable to no one, not even the Great Council. The Procurator was the "Custodian of St Mark", of the wealth that accumulated in the coffers of the Basilica di San Marco (see entry) as a result of public and private gifts, bequests and regular income. The sums in question were enormous, since a donation was always made to St Mark as a matter of course in thanksgiving for a successful and profitable enterprise.

It was with this huge fortune that the State financed all that it owned, the construction of San Marco and every one of its welfare institutions: hospitals, alms distribution, hostels for the homeless, homes for the aged and orphanages – institutions that guaranteed even the poorest the means of subsistence.

It soon became impossible for one person to shoulder alone the burden of the work that came to be involved in administering the public purse; in the 13th c. there were four Procurators, in 1319 six, and in 1442 nine.

As early as 1204 there was a two-storey building on the present-day site of the Procuratie Vecchie. The present three-storey building dates from between 1480 and 1517; the architect was Mauro Coducci and the building work was completed by Bartolomeo Bon. It is a very fine example of Venetian Early Renaissance architecture and has arcades along the length of its façade – 150 m (164 yds) – 50 on the ground floor and 100 on each of the upper storeys.

Procuratie Vecchie
(Old Procurators' Offices)
(N side of the Piazza)

When even the enlarged Procuratie Vecchie became too small the Procuratie Nuove were begun in 1582 on the S side of the Piazza di San Marco. The architect Vincenzo Scamozzi used Sansovino's library as a model; he merely added another storey and topped it with a cornice (instead of a balustrade). Baldassare Longhena completed the building in 1640 in accordance with Scamozzi's original plans.

Procuratie Nuove
(New Procurators' Offices)
(S side of the Piazza)

Today the former official residence of the Procurators houses the Museo Civico Correr, where the magnificent official robes of the Procurators can be admired, the Museo del Risorgimento and the Museo Archeologico (see entries).

Between 1805 and 1814 Napoleon lived in the Procuratie Nuove whenever, in his capacity as "King of Italy", he visited Venice, his second Italian seat of residence after Milan.

Raccolta Peggy Guggenheim (Peggy Guggenheim Collection)

See Ca' Venier dei Leoni

Il Redentore (church)

See La Giudecca, Il Redentore

Rialto Bridge

See Ponte di Rialto

San Bartolomeo (church)   K4

This was the guild church of the German merchants in Venice for which Albrecht Dürer painted his famous "Feast of the Rosary" (1506), later acquired by Emperor Rudolf II and taken to Prague (where it is still to be found).

Location
Campo San Bartolomeo

Quay
Rialto

In the choir of the church are the paintings of four saints executed by Sebastiano del Piombo (c. 1485–1547) as shutters for the organ. The altar-piece on the High Altar, "The Martyrdom of St Bartholomew" by Palma the Younger, is also of interest.

Opening times
Mon.–Sat. 9–11 a.m.

Temporarily closed

San Francesco del Deserto (island)

Quay
San Francesco del Deserto
(from Riva degli Schiavoni)

Opening times
8 a.m.–noon and 2.30–
3.30 p.m. daily

According to legend St Francis of Assisi rested on this tiny island on his way back from the Holy Land (1220). The little church dating from 1228, surrounded by cypresses, has a magical atmosphere. After a visit it is customary to give the monks a small donation.

San Francesco della Vigna (church)   N4

Location
Campo San Francesco della
Vigna

Quay
San Zaccaria

Work on this large church was begun by Sansovino in 1534. It was not completed until 40 years later when Andrea Palladio assumed the main responsibility for the façade (1568–72).
The church contains some interesting paintings. In the S transept is an important panel-painting, "The Virgin adoring the Infant Jesus" (*c.* 1450) by Antonio da Negroponte. The Capella Santa (access from the N transept) has a "Madonna and Saints" by Giovanni Bellini (1507), one of his late works. In the Sacristy is a triptych by Antonio Vivarini (15th c.) and in the fifth chapel on the left a "Madonna" by Paolo Veronese (1551).
Also interesting is a 15th c. series of sculptures by Pietro Lombardo in the Cappella Giustiniani (to the left of the High Altar).

San Giacomo dell'Orio (church)   H4

Location
Campo San Giacomo
dell'Orio

Quay
San Staè

The church and its Romanesque Campanile date back in their present form to the 16th c. The Presbytery was not added until the early 16th c.
It has a richly carved wooden ceiling. The altar-piece in the choir – "Madonna and four Saints" (1546) – by Lorenzo Lotto is especially interesting. The Old Sacristy contains works by Palma the Younger.

* San Giobbe (church)   F2

Location
Campo San Giobbe

Quay
Ferrovia (railway station)

The Church of San Giobbe is the first example of Tuscan Renaissance architecture in Venice. It was built by Antonio Gambello (from 1450) who began the church in the Late Gothic style (the Campanile is of that period) and Pietro Lombardo (from 1471).
Especially interesting are Paris Bordone's "SS Andrew, Peter and Nicholas" dating from the 16th c. (fourth side-altar on the right), Girolamo Savoldo's "Nativity" in the Cappelle Contarini, and the fine tomb-slab of Doge Cristoforo Moro (the church's founder) and his wife Cristina Sanudo, dated 1471, which is in front of the High Altar. In the Cappella Da Mula is a triptych by Antonio Vivarini (*c.* 1445) which can be seen on request.
The way to the church is along the Canale di Cannaregio and then left at the bridge, the Ponte del Tre Archi.

Island and Church of San Giorgio Maggiore

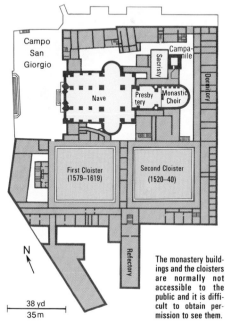

San Giorgio Maggiore

Of special interest within the church:

S aisle
On the second altar a splendid wooden Crucifix (late 15th c.)
On the third altar a painting from the school of Tintoretto, "The Martyrdom of St Cosmas and St Damian"

N aisle
On the second altar a marble sculpture by Girolamo Campagna (1595)

S transept
Altarpiece from Tintoretto's studio, "The Coronation of the Virgin" (1594)

N transept
"The Martyrdom of St Stephen" by Tintoretto

Presbytery
At the front two bronze candelsticks dated 1598. "The Shower of Manna" and "The Last Supper" (1594) by Tintoretto

Monastic Choir
Splendid Baroque stalls

High Altar
Bronze sculpture by Girolamo Campagna (late 16th c.)

The monastery buildings and the cloisters are normally not accessible to the public and it is difficult to obtain permission to see them.

San Giorgio Maggiore (island)   L/M6/7

Quay
San Giorgio

The American writer Henry James once wrote of the island that it has "a success beyond all reason". The island owes its beauty mainly to its position and to the genius of the Venetian architects. The first church was built in 790 and 200 years later the Benedictine monastery was added. Both buildings were destroyed by an earthquake. The monastery was rebuilt and in the 16th c. San Giorgio Maggiore was built on the site of the old church. After the Second World War the buildings on the island became increasingly dilapidated until finally the Italian industrialist Vittorio Cini set up the Giorgio Cini Foundation in memory of his son Giorgio. This foundation financed the restoration of dilapidated or decaying buildings and built an International Centre of Art and Culture with 30 auditoria, a cinema, an open-air theatre and a naval college.

In 1980 the Western Heads of State met on San Giorgio Maggiore for the famous Venice economic summit conference.

*San Giorgio Maggiore (church)

Quay
San Giorgio

Opening times
Campanile: 9 a.m.–
12.30 p.m., 2.30–6 or 7 p.m.
daily

The first Church of San Giorgio Maggiore was built here about 790. The present building dates from 1565–76. It was begun by Andrea Palladio, but was not completed until 1610, 30 years after his death, by Scamozzi. A bell-tower was built in 1470 but the present one dates from the 18th c. It is well worth going up the tower (lift) since from the platform there is a marvellous panoramic view of the city and the lagoon (entrance to the left of the monastic choir).

The most important paintings in the church are Tintoretto's "The Shower of Manna" and "The Last Supper" in the Presbytery. The High Altar is the work of Girolamo Campagna, a pupil of Sansovino (late 16th c.).

San Giovanni in Bragora (church)   M5

Location
Campo Bandiera e Moro

Quay
Arsenale

This church is one of the oldest in Venice and was founded as early as the 7th c. It was built in its present Late-Gothic style in 1475 and the Presbytery was added in 1485–94.

Inside are three masterpieces of early Venetian painting. In the apse of the choir is Cima da Conegliano's "Baptism of Christ" (1494) in a marble frame, one of the master's finest works. In the left choir chapel is a triptych by Bartolomeo Vivarini, "The Madonna Enthroned between St John the Baptist and St Andrew" (1478). In the first side-chapel on the left (next to the entrance) is a "Resurrection" by Alvise Vivarini (1498), an Early Renaissance work.

Over the entrance is an interesting work by Palma Giovane, "Christ before Caiaphas" (1600).

San Giovanni Crisostomo (church)   K4

Quay
Rialto

This domed Renaissance-style church, in the form of a Greek cross, is one of the masterpieces of Mauro Coducci who built it between 1497 and 1504 on the foundations of an earlier church. It is dedicated to St Chrysostom.

Of interest in the interior are a late work by Giovanni Bellini, "St Jerome, St Christopher and St Augustine" (1513; first side chapel on the right) and, over the High Altar, "Madonna and Saints" (including St Chrysostom; 1509–11) by Sebastiano del Piombo.

Also of interest is the marble bas-relief "The Coronation of the Virgin" (1500–02) by Tullio Lombardo on the second altar on the left.

San Marcuola (officially: Santi Ermagora e Fortunato; church)   H3

The Church of San Marcuola was built between 1728 and 1736 by the architect Giorgio Massari, but the façade overlooking the Canal Grande was never completed.

The most important works of art in the interior are Tintoretto's "The Last Supper" (1547; Presbytery, left-hand wall) and an old copy of his "Washing of the feet" (opposite). It is also worth noting that the altars are richly decorated not with paintings but with sculptures.

Location
Campo San Marcuola

Quay
San Marcuola

San Michele (island)   M/N1/2

San Michele is the cemetery island of Venice. The present cemetery was laid out in the 19th c. Since it is on an island, the cemetery's capacity is limited and most Venetians can only count on having a resting-place there for 12 years, after which remains are reinterred communally and burial-places are reused. Serge Diaghilev is buried in the Orthodox section of the cemetery.

Of the monastery that used to be here there remains the 15th c. cloister, together with the attractive Renaissance Church of San Michele, built by Mauro Coducci (1469–78).

The hexagonal Cappella Emiliana added by Guglielmo Bergamasco in 1530 is also worth seeing.

Quay
San Michele (Line 5 from Fondamenta Nuove, or Riva degli Schiavoni)

San Moisè (church)   K5/6

Art connoisseurs find the Baroque façade of the church (built by Alessandro Tremignon in 1668) too rich and over-ornate. But the Venetians love their "San Moisè" with its typical Venetian bell-tower.

Worth seeing in the interior are a "Pietà" dating from 1732 (interior wall of the façade), a bronze relief of the Deposition (designed by the Roccatagliata brothers in 1633; Sacristy altar) and the Baroque sculpture on the High Altar of Moses receiving the Tablets on Mount Sinai (by the Austrian Meyring).

Location
Calle Largo 22 Marzo

Quay
San Marco

San Nicolò (church)

The church dates back to 1044 but was reconstructed in the Baroque style in the 17th c. and has an unfinished façade.

Location
Lido

San Pietro di Castello

Quay
San Nicolò

It was once thought that this church contained the remains of St Nicholas that Venetian sailors had stolen from the cathedral of the town on Myra (which belonged at that time to the Byzantine Empire) on the S coast of Asia Minor (opposite Rhodes). Some time after this had been celebrated and the monastery and the church had been founded the Venetians discovered that the people of Bari in Apulia had beaten them to it; they had made away with the remains of the "real" St Nicholas.

The cloister and paintings by Palma the Elder and Palma the Younger are especially interesting.

San Pietro di Castello (church)   Q5

Location
Campo San Pietro

On the island of San Pietro di Castello, on the E edge of the city and on the site of one of the first settlements in the lagoon, that of Olivolo, this church was built to serve Venice as its first cathedral.

Quay
Giardini

According to legend in the 7th c. Bishop Magnus of Altinum had a vision of St Peter who ordered him to build a church "where he found sheep and goats grazing". From 775 onwards the Church of San Pietro was the episcopal church and from 1451 to 1807 it was the church of the Patriarchs of Venice. This function was not taken over by the Basilica di San Marco (see entry) until after the fall of the Republic.

The present church was built in the 17th c. Its façade is thought to be based on a design by Palladio. The Campanile was designed by Mauro Coducci (1482–88) in the Early Renaissance style. The original tower roof collapsed in 1670.

Of interest are the Baroque High Altar by Baldassare Longhena (1649) and the so-called "Cattedra di San Pietro", the marble throne supposed to have been used by St Peter in Antioch.

San Polo (officially: San Paolo; church)   H4

Location
Campo San Polo

Quay
San Silvestro

The original Late Gothic church, founded in the 9th c. was reconstructed and drastically altered in the 19th c.; the Campanile (14th c.) has survived unaltered.

Of interest inside is "The Last Supper" that Tintoretto painted in 1568–69 (it is his second version of the theme; another "Last Supper" by Tintoretto dating from 1547 is in the Church of San Marcuola (see entry) while a third version, which he painted when he was much older, can be seen in San Giorgio Maggiore; see entry). Also of interest are the bronze statue near the High Altar by Alessandro Vittoria and G. B. Tiepolo's painting "Madonna with St John of Nepomuk".

The Oratory of the Crucifix contains G. D. Tiepolo's "Stations of the Cross".

San Salvatore (church)   K5

The 7th c. church was reconstructed between 1506 and 1534
by Giorgio Spavento, Tullio Lombardo and Sansovino and
given its present Baroque façade by Giuseppe Sardi between
1663 and 1700. There is reason to suppose that its creators
intended that San Salvatore should rival the Basilica di San
Marco (see entry) in its size and splendour, but it has only three
domes as compared with the five of San Marco.
The interior has retained its Renaissance style and houses
several important works of art. The baldachins give the
impression of great spaciousness.
The most interesting of the monuments is the splendid
memorial to Doge Francesco Venier, designed by Sansovino
(1556–61; past the second altar on the left).
The outstanding paintings are the two works by Titian: "The
Annunciation" (third altar on the right, with a marble frame by
Sansovino) and "The Transfiguration of Christ" (on the High
Altar). Another interesting painting, "The Supper of Ammaus",
by Giovanni Bellini (or his school) is on the wall of the left choir
chapel.

Location
Calle Mazzini

Quay
Rialto

* San Sabastiano (church)   F6

The Renaissance Church of San Sebastiano was built between
1505 and 1546. This is where Paolo Veronese who decorated
the interior almost single-handed is buried (on the left of the
choir). Numbered among his most important works is "The
Coronation of the Virgin" and on the ceiling in the Sacristy are
the four panels of the Evangelists which made his reputation
(entrance under the organ). On the ceiling of the nave are
Veronese's scenes from the Life of Esther: "Esther taken before
Ahasuerus", "Esther crowned Queen", "The Triumph of
Mordecai". The splendid frames of the ceiling-paintings are
also interesting.
The wall-paintings (also in the nave) are by Paolo Veronese
and his brother Benedetto. The organ-case was also designed
and painted by Paolo Veronese.
In 1565 in the Nun's Choir he painted the frescoes "St
Sebastian before Diocletian" and "The Martyrdom of St
Sebastian".
On the High Altar is one of the artist's later works, "Madonna
in Majesty with SS Sebastian, Peter, Catherine and Francis".

Location
Campo San Sebastiano

Quay
Ca' Rezzonico

San Staè (officially: Sant'Eustachio; church)   H3

The church was built in 1678 by Giovanni Grassi and is in
the shape of a Greek cross. The façade on the Grand Canal
was added thirty years later (1709) by the master-builder
Domenico Rossi.
The interior is decorated with early 18th c. works, including
G. B. Piazzetta's "The Martyrdom of St James the Great",
Sebastiano Ricci's "The Freeing of St Peter", "The Torment of
St Bartholomew" by G. B. Tiepolo, and "The Crucifixion of St
Andrew" by G. A. Pellegrini.

Location
Campo San Staè/
Canal Grande

Quay
San Staè

San Trovaso (officially: Santi Gervasio e Protasio; church)   G6

Location
Campo San Trovaso

Quay
Accademia

This church is in fact dedicated to SS Gervase and Protase but their names were finally abbreviated to Trovaso. The interior is simple but it has several paintings by well-known artists: Tintoretto's "The Last Supper" (left transept) and "The Temptation of St Antony" (left choir chapel), and "St Chrysogonus" by Michele Giambono (right choir chapel). The most important works of art in the church are the marble altar reliefs (right transept) by an unknown artist. They are thought to date from about 1470.

San Zaccaria (church)   L/M5

Location
Campo San Zaccaria

Quay
San Zaccaria

This church was probably founded in the 9th c. The present church was built between 1444 and 1500 by the two great master-builders Antonio Gambello and Mauro Coducci. The huge façade is an astounding example of the transition from Gothic to Early Renaissance architecture – a successful compromise. Unfortunately the interior is fraught with hostility which sometimes manifests itself in open warfare – a devastating clash of styles.

Of especial interest are Giovanni Bellini's altar-piece "Virgin and Child with SS Peter, Catherine, Lucy and Jerome" dating from 1505 (second side-altar on the left) and Andrea del Castagno's frescoes (1452) in the groined Gothic vault of the Cappella di San Tarasio.

San Zaccaria was considered the rowdiest of all the convents in the rowdy city of 18th c. Venice. The riotous parties held in the convent and the love-affairs indulged in by the nuns were the talk of the town. This was because most of San Zaccaria's nuns were the daughters of noble families, sent there against their will, to save the expense of dowries. Cheated out of their lives, they found their own way of avenging themselves.

Santa Maria della Fava (church)   K4

Location
Calle della Fava

Quay
Rialto

This 18th c. church has a single nave lined by reliefs and statues by Giuseppe Bernardi, the teacher of Antonio Canova. It also contains an early work by G. B. Tiepolo, "The Education of the Virgin" (1732; first side-chapel on the right) and a masterpiece by G. B. Piazzetta, "The Virgin and Child with St Philip Neri" (1725–27; second side altar on the left).

*Santa Maria Formosa (church)   L4/5

Location
Campo Santa Maria Formosa

Quay
Rialto

Mauro Coducci built this church in 1492 on the foundations of an older, probably 11th c. church (the façade overlooking the Campo and the Baroque bell-tower were added in the 17th c.). The result was an extremely successful merging of a basic Byzantine shape and Venetian Renaissance architecture, and an interior which, with its slender columns, little cupolas and

Santa Maria Formosa and market-place

barrel-vaults, gives the impression of being Byzantine yet is smothered with marvellous Renaissance ornamentation.

The most interesting works of art are Bartolomeo Vivarini's altar-piece "Madonna of Mercy" (1473) and Palma the Elder's altar-piece (1522–24) in the Cappella della Scuola degli Artiglieri (Chapel of the Guild of Artillerymen) which in the centre features an heroic St Barbara, Patron Saint of Gunners. Every morning the square round the church, the Campo Santa Maria Formosa, is the scene of the picturesque fruit market.

Until the fall of the Republic it was traditional for the Doge to visit the church every year at Candlemas. This was because one day in 944 a number of girls on their way to church were abducted by Slavs from Dalmatia. They were rescued by the Scuola dei Casselleri (Guild of the Makers of Marriage Coffers), who had their oratory in the church. As their reward the Doge was asked to make an annual visit to the church at Candlemas. "But what shall I do if it rains?" asked the Doge. "We shall give you a hat." "And what shall I do if I am thirsty?" "We shall give you wine." From then on every year at Candlemas the Doge was given a straw hat and a flagon of wine at the Church of Santa Maria Formosa. One of the hats can be seen in the Museo Correr (see entry).

---

*Santa Maria dei Miracoli (church)   K/L4

Santa Maria dei Miracoli is a masterpiece of Early Renaissance architecture, built by Pietro Lombardo (1481–89) to enshrine a miraculous picture of the Virgin. Instead of decorating the

Location
Calle delle Erbe

Santa Maria della Salute

Santa Maria della Salute

Quay
Rialto

exterior with sculpture he used cleverly matched coloured marble arranged to form rosettes, circles, octagons and crosses on the façade. The interior is embellished in the same way, with the golden domes ceiling achieving a much greater effect above the grey and coral marble walls as a result. Steps lead from the nave to the chancel which is partitioned off by an exquisite Early Renaissance balustrade with figures of St Francis, the Archangel Gabriel, the Virgin and St Clare. This interior is one of the most beautiful in all Venice.

* Santa Maria della Salute (church)   J6

Location
Fondamenta Salute

Quay
Salute

This Baroque domed church was built to commemorate the plague which in 1630 claimed over 40,000 victims in Venice alone. Baldassare Longhena began the work in 1631 on foundations of over 1 million wooden piles. It was not completed until 1687, five years after his death. Longhena's design was only accepted by the Senate because it "would make a grand impression without costing too much".

The Church of Our Lady depicts Mary as "Ruler of the Sea" (Capitana del Mar); the statue of the Virgin on the top of the dome carries the staff of command of a Venetian Admiral of the Fleet.

The broad flight of steps leading up to the church and its two huge domes not only give it an astounding breadth but also enhance the whole cityscape. Seen from the sea (the true "view of Venice") Santa Maria della Salute perfectly offsets the Basilica di San Marco, the Doges' Palace (Palazzo Ducale) and the Campanile (see entries). In the last few decades it has been severely damaged by pollution, as has almost the whole city. In recent years it has been restored with money provided by the French Save Venice Fund.

The interior is rather austere. Of the many sculptures (there are over 120 in all) the group on the High Altar by Juste Le Court is probably the most important: the Madonna complying with the fervent request of Venezia and driving out the plague. The faithful commemorate the end of the plague and the founding of the church by holding a solemn service and procession every year on 21 November, the Feast of the Salvation.

The paintings in the Great Sacristy are also interesting: Tintoretto's "Marriage at Cana" (1561; long wall) and Titian's ceiling-paintings "Cain and Abel", "The Sacrifice of Abraham" and "David and Goliath" (1542–44). The altar-piece "St Mark Enthroned with four Saints" is also by Titian.

To the left of the church is the Seminario Patriarcale which houses the Manfredinian Picture Gallery (see Seminario e Pinacoteca Manfrediniana).

Santa Maria Zobenigo (officially: Santa Maria del Giglio; church)   J6

The church was founded in the 9th c. by the Zubanico family and so it got its name, but it is usually called Santa Maria del Giglio. The interior was restored in 1660 and the Baroque façade was added in 1678–83 by Giuseppe Sardi on the orders of Antonio Barbaro who as a quid pro quo ensured his own immortality by having a stone statue of himself placed above the main portal with, underneath, some of his ancestors. The lower plinths are decorated with reliefs showing panoramas of the cities in which Antonio Barbaro had served: Padua, Candia (Crete), Zara (left), Rome, Corfu and Spalato (right).

The Sacristy contains an early work by Tintoretto, "The Four Evangelists" (1552–57).

Location
Campo Santa Maria del Giglio

Quay
San Marco

Santi Apostoli (church)   K4

This 14th c. church (reconstructed 16th–18th c.) is really only of interest because of the superb Corner family chapel (on the right of the nave), attributed to Mauro Coducci in the late 15th c. It is one of the finest examples of Venetian Renaissance architecture (it was originally intended as the burial-place of the Queen of Cyprus). The richly carved columns and the delicate cupola achieve an astonishing harmony.

Giambattista Tiepolo's altar-piece, "The Communion of St Lucy" (1746–48) is radiantly beautiful.

Location
Campo dei Santi Apostoli

Quay
Ca' d'Oro

Santi Giovanni e Paolo

See Zanipolo

Santo Stefano (church)   H/J5

Location
Campo Morosoni

Quay
Accademia

The Late Gothic church at the top end of the Campo Morosoni dates from 1374. The perilously crooked Campanile, the gables on the façade, the choir and the wooden vault in the nave (a splendid piece of work) were added 150 years later.

Two important Venetians are buried in the simple interior. In the nave is the tomb-slab of Doge Francesco Morosoni who recaptured the Peloponnese for Venice but at the same time blew up the Parthenon on the Acropolis with a single shot (it was used by the Turks to store their gunpowder).

Giovanni Gabriele (1557–1612) is buried in front of the first altar on the left. The composer was Organist at San Marco (see Basilica di San Marco) and a pioneer of Early Baroque music. Santo Stefano also contains several valuable paintings by Venetian artists. These include Tintoretto's "The Last Supper", "Christ Washing the Disciples' Feet" and "The Agony in the Garden" in the Sacristy and Nicolò Bambini's "The Birth of the Virgin" on the first altar on the right.

Apart from the paintings the Late Gothic choir-stalls in the Presbytery and the fragments of a parclose (both 1488) are also interesting.

The fine monastery cloister restored in 1532 (entrance at the E end of the N aisle) contain frescoes by Pordenone, in a ruinous state, unfortunately.

Scuola dei Carmini (confraternity house of the Carmelites)   F5

Location
Campo Santa Margherita

Quay
Ca' Rezzonico

Opening times
Mon.–Sat. 9 a.m.–noon,
2–5 p.m., Sun. 9 a.m.–noon

Admission charge

This Scuola formerly served one of the six most important confraternities of Venice. The Scuole were not schools but meeting-places and houses of prayer for religious fraternities in which Venetian citizens banded together. They were organised either according to country of origin or according to occupation, had specific religious or charitable aims and above all provided mutual assistance and charitable benefits. They were often very rich, and this is demonstrated by their splendid confraternity houses.

The Scuola dei Carmini belonged to a lay confraternity of Carmelites who, nevertheless, were able to commission such important artists as Giambattista Tiepolo and Nicolò Bambini to decorate their house for them. In the hall on the upper floor G. B. Tiepolo did nine ceiling-paintings between 1739 and 1744, including his most mature work "Mary handing St Simon Stock the Scapular of the Carmelites". Tiepolo was paid only 400 sequins for this fresco.

The other paintings, all dating from the 18th c., are also interesting, and include some by Nicolò Bambini.

Scuola Grande di San Marco (confraternity house of San Marco)   L4

Location
Campo SS Giovanni e Paolo

Quay
Rialto

The Scuola Grande di San Marco, adjoining the Church of Santi Giovanni e Paolo (see Zanipolo), served the rich confraternity of goldsmiths and silk-merchants. Today it is a municipal hospital. The lower part of the building was begun about 1485 by Pietro Lombardo; his son Tullio did the reliefs and the two lions. Mauro Coducci finally completed the building in about 1495 by adding the upper part with its stepped round gables crowned with figures.

Although not as clear-cut as Santa Maria dei Miracoli nor as forceful as San Zaccaria (see entries), the splendid façade is, nevertheless, one of the outstanding examples of Venetian Renaissance architecture. The "trompe-l'œil" effects on the ground floor, the fluid arches and the sculptuary on the gables combine to fine effect.

The sculpture in the lunette of the doorway "St Mark with the Brethren of the Scuola" is attributed to Bartolomeo Bon. Bon also worked on the Porta della Carta in the Doges' Palace (see Palazzo Ducale).

Opening times
Mon.–Sat. 9 a.m.–1 p.m.,
3.30–6.30 p.m.
Sun. and public holidays
9 a.m.–1 p.m.

---

*Scuola Grande di San Rocco (confraternity house of San Rocco) G4/5

This impressive white marble building was constructed between 1515 and 1560 to a design by Bartolomeo Bon. The Scuola has become world-famous because of its series of paintings by the great 16th c. artist Tintoretto.

Ground floor
Eight large paintings by the Master with scenes from the Life of the Virgin, including "The Annunciation", "The Flight into Egypt" and "The Massacre of the Innocents".

Upper floor
The large hall has ceiling- and wall-paintings executed by Tintoretto between 1575 and 1581 depicting episodes from the Old and New Testaments with the latter echoing the former – "The Miracle of Manna" remembered in "Christ Feeding the Five Thousand".

The works in the Committee Room (Sala dell'Albergo) date back to 1564 and 1567, and includes "The Glorification of St Roch", "Christ before Pilate", the "Ecce Homo", and, above all, "that vast and terrible picture 'The Crucifixion'", to quote Edward Hutton, a picture which Ruskin thought "beyond all analysis and above all praise".

Location
Campo San Rocco

Quay
San Tomà

Opening times
10 a.m.–1 p.m. daily and
3–6 p.m. on Sat. and Sun.

Scuola di San Giorgio degli Schiavoni M5
(confraternity house of St George of the Dalmatians)

This was the Scuola of the Dalmatian merchants, the "Schiavoni" (Slavs). Between 1502 and 1507 Vittore Carpaccio decorated its walls with the cycle of paintings which still survive complete and which rank as his most important work alongside his pictures in the Galleria dell'Accademia, the Museo Correr and the Ca' d'Oro (see entries).

There are no captions to the pictures. Those on the left wall are "St George killing the Dragon" and "The Triumph of St George".

Left and right of the altar: "St George baptising the heathen King and Queen" and "St Tryphon exorcising the Daughter of the Emperor Gordianus".

Location
Calle dei Furlani

Quay
San Zaccaria

Opening times
Tues.–Sat. 10 a.m.–
12.30 p.m., 3.30–6 p.m.,
Sun. 10.30 a.m.–12.30 p.m.

Closed
Mon.

93

Admission charge

Right wall: "The Agony in the Garden", "The Calling of St Matthew", "St Jerome leading his Lion into a Monastery", "The Funeral of St Jerome", and the remarkable "St Augustine in his Study".

Seminario e Pinacoteca Manfrediniana   J/K6
(seminary building and art gallery)

Location
Fondamenta Salute

Quay
Salute

Opening times
By appointment only

The Seminario Patriarcale to the left of the Church of Santa Maria della Salute (see entry) houses the Pinacoteca Manfrediniana. Seminario and church were both designed by Longhena (1669).
The art collection of Marquis Federico Manfredini of Florence contains terracotta busts by Alessandro Vittoria (1525–1608), paintings by Antonio Vivarini (15th c.), Cima da Conegliano, Konrad Laib and Filippini Lippi; a major work by Antonio Canova (1757–1822; a bust of Gian Matteo Amadei) and a ceiling-painting in the library, "Glory of the Sciences" (c. 1720), by Sebastiano Ricci.

Bridge of Sighs

See Palazzo Ducale, Ponte dei Sospiri

* Teatro La Fenice (La Fenice theatre)   J5

Location
Calle delle Veste

Quay
San Marco

Season
November–July

The Teatro La Fenice is the opera-house of Venice. Built between 1790 and 1792, it was rebuilt in its original Neo-Classical style in 1836 after a fire.
Its interior is richly decorated with gold, pink and white stucco, carvings and gilding. Rossini, Bellini and Verdi composed operas specially for this splendid theatre which thus saw the first performances of Verdi's operas "Ernani" (1844), "Rigoletto" (1851), "La Traviata" (1853) and "Simon Boccanegra" (1857). It also staged the première of Benjamin Britten's "The Turn of the Screw".
Incidentally, the rapturous reception for Verdi and the incessant chants of "Viva Verdi" were not simply on grounds of artistic merit. VERDI spelt out the clarion call of Italian opposition to Austrian rule and stood for Vittorio Emanuele Re D'Italia (Victor Emanuel, King of Italy).

* Torcello (island)

Quay
Torcello (Line 12 from Fondamenta Nuove)

Opening times
Cathedral: 10 a.m.–
12.30 p.m., 1.30–6 p.m. daily

Torcello is the real precursor of Venice. It was founded on the island as early as the 7th c. and in the 12th c. was a flourishing commercial town with palaces and churches, shipyards and docks, its own nobility, its own laws and a large population. The large town has vanished, leaving only two churches and a handful of houses dotted over this large island; the growth of Venice and malaria were responsible for this diminution. The cathedral serves as the main proof of its former importance.

Santa Maria Assunta (cathedral)

Dedicated in 639 to "Santa Maria Assunta", the cathedral is probably the best example of the Venetian-Byzantine style of architecture. Reconstructed in 834 and 1008, the portico and the two lateral apses were added in the 9th c. and the main fabric of the building dates from the 11th c.
The cathedral contains some beautiful mosaics.

Right side-chapels

Interior of the cathedral

The oldest mosaics are in the chapel to the right of the High Altar. The angels carrying a medallion with the Lamb of God are still strongly marked by Byzantine influence (11th c.; vaulting of the apse). The Fathers of the Church, Gregory, Martin, Ambrose and Augustine were added later, as was the Christ in Majesty between two Archangels (concha of the apse).

Main apse
The mosaics in the main apse date from the 12th c.: the Virgin and Child above a frieze of the Twelve Apostles standing among flowers, all on a gold ground.

W side
The W wall of the cathedral is covered by the tiers of a Byzantine mosaic of the Last Judgment dating from the late 12th or early 13th c.
Top tier: Christ at the shattered gates of Limbo.
Second tier: Christ as Judge of the World.
Third tier: Christ enthroned with the Archangels Michael and Gabriel, and Adam and Eve (kneeling); also angels sounding the trumpets heralding the Last Judgment (at the sides).
On either side of the door: the Blessed (clothed), the Damned (naked).

Other points of interest:

The rood-screen
A series of 15th c. panel-paintings of the Virgin and the Twelve Apostles is supported by marble panels carved with reliefs of peacocks and lions (11th c.).

The High Altar
This dates from the 7th c. and was restored in the early 20th c. Also of interest are the iconostasis (15th c.), the mosaic floor (11th c.) and the pulpit (assembled in the 13th c. from earlier fragments).

The small Church of Saint Fosca adjoining the cathedral is centrally planned and purely Byzantine. Dating from the 11th c., it has a portico on five sides and its interior is of unusually harmonious proportions.

Santa Fosca (church)

Torre dell'Orologio (clock tower)   K5

The clock tower was designed and built (1496–99) by Mauro Coducci, probably to finish off the Procuratie Vecchie (see entry). It is typical of Venetian Renaissance architecture.
The top storey with the mosaic of gold stars strewn over a blue background and the Lion of St Mark were added in 1755 by Giorgio Massari.

Location
Piazza di San Marco

Quay
San Marco

San Zanipolo
Santi Giovanni e Paolo

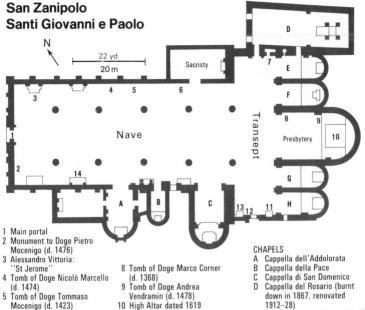

1 Main portal
2 Monument to Doge Pietro
   Mocenigo (d. 1476)
3 Alessandro Vittoria:
   "St Jerome"
4 Tomb of Doge Nicolò Marcello
   (d. 1474)
5 Tomb of Doge Tommaso
   Mocenigo (d. 1423)
6 Monument to Doge Pasquale
   Malipiero (d. 1462)
7 Monument to Doge Sebastiano
   Venier (d. 1578)

8 Tomb of Doge Marco Corner
   (d. 1368)
9 Tomb of Doge Andrea
   Vendramin (d. 1478)
10 High Altar dated 1619
11 Altar-piece by Rocco Marconi
12 Altar-piece by Lorenzo Lotto
13 Panel by A. Vivarini
14 Altar with panel by Giovanni Bellini

CHAPELS
A Cappella dell'Addolorata
B Cappella della Pace
C Cappella di San Domenico
D Cappella del Rosario (burnt
   down in 1867, renovated
   1912–28)
E Cappella Cavalli (di San Pio V)
F Cappella della Trinità
G Cappella della Maddalena
H Cappella del Crocifisso

The two bronze Mori Moors on the terrace who strike the bell to mark the hours were cast by Paolo Ranieri (1494–97). Visitors can climb up to the roof of the clock tower to get a closer view of these two figures.

The magnificent great clock (from which the tower gets its name) was also made by Ranieri and his son. It shows the hours, the phases of the moon and the signs of the zodiac. Above the clock-face is a gilded Madonna. During Ascension Week and at Epiphany the Three Kings are conducted by an angel past the Madonna at each hour.

Below the clock tower is the passage leading to the shopping street of the Merceria (see entry).

Opening times
Tues.–Sat. 9 a.m.–noon,
3–5 p.m., July and August
3–6 p.m. Sun. and public
holidays 9 a.m.–noon

Closed
Mon.

Admission charge

Zanipolo (officially: Santi Giovanni e Paolo; Dominican church)   L4

Next to the Franciscan Church of I Frari (see entry), the church of the Mendicant Order of Dominicans, the Zanipolo, is the prime example of Late Gothic ecclesiastical architecture in

Location
Campo SS Giovanni e Paolo

◄ *Torre dell'Orologio: clock tower with bronze Moors and the Lion of St Mark*

Venice. The vast brick structure, begun in 1246 and consecrated in 1430, is sometimes justifiably referred to as the "Pantheon of the Doges". Twenty-five Doges were buried here and after the 15th c. all funerals of Doges were held here. Many of their tombs were designed by Pietro Lombardo, the architect of the Church of Santa Maria dei Miracoli (see entry), and his equally famous son Tullio.

Interior of the church

Tombs

Of especial interest are that masterpiece of the Renaissance, the tomb of Doge Andrea Vendramin (d. 1478), by Tullio and Antonio Lombardo (1492–95; in the left of the presbytery) and the monument to Doge Pietro Mocenigo (d. 1476), a remarkably fine work by Pietro Lombardo (1481; to the right of the entrance), which bears reliefs of his most famous victories; the inscription is a reminder that the monument was set up at the expense of his enemies.

Capilla del Rosario

Formerly decorated with Titian's "St Peter Martyr" and works by Tintoretto and Palma the Younger, all destroyed in the fire of 1867. The ceiling has paintings by Veronese brought here from the ex-church of the Umiltà: "The Adoration of the Magi" (in the Presbytery), "The Assumption of the Virgin" (at the front of the chapel), "The Adoration of the Shepherds", "The Annunication" and "The Nativity" (on the wall by the entrance).

High Altar

The High Altar is thought to have been designed by Baldassare Longhena in about 1619. Its Baroque design was used as a model for altars in southern Germany and Austria.

S transept

"St Antonius Pieruzzi giving Alms" (1542) is the work of Lorenzo Lotto (St Antonius Pieruzzi was Archbishop of Florence). The stained glass in the window above it is from Murano and represents figures from the Bible, the Early Fathers and Dominican saints.

On the wall next to the Cappella San Domenico is a work by Alvise Vivarini entitled "Bearing the Cross".

In the Cappella San Domenico is G. B. Piazetta's ceiling-painting "The Glory of St Dominic".

S aisle

The Early Renaissance Polyptych of the Life of St Vincent Ferrer (still in its original frame) is by Giovanni Bellini (c. 1465).

Practical Information

Airlines

Campo San Moisè 1463; tel 70 03 55.   Alitalia

Riva degli Schiavoni 4158; tel. 850 26.   British Airways

General Sales, 14075 San Marco; tel 70 32 19, 70 32 30.   TWA

Banks

Open Mon.–Fri. 8.30 a.m.–12.30 or 1.30 p.m.   Opening times

S.V.E.T. (Soc. Viaggi e Turismo),
San Marco 145a (Piazza).
Open Mon.–Sat. 9 a.m.–12.30 p.m. Sun., public holidays
9 a.m.–12.30 p.m., 2.30–6.30 p.m.

American Express,
San Marco 1474 (San Moisè).
Open Mon.–Fri. 8.45 a.m.–5 p.m., Sat. 8.45 a.m.–12.30 p.m.

American Express Bank,
San Marco 1336.
Open Mon.–Fri. 8.30 a.m.–1.30 p.m.

Banca Nazionale del Lavorno (Bureau de change),
Rio Terrà A. Foscarini 877/d (near the Accademia).
Open Mon.–Fri. 8.30 a.m.–1.30 p.m.

Banca Nazionale delle Comunicazioni,
Stazione San Lucia (railway station).
Open also on Sun. and public holidays.

Most banks in the city centre will cash Eurocheques. Since   Eurocheques
each bank may quote a different rate it is worth while
comparing rates.

Caution is necessary in dealing with small street exchange   Bureaux de change
offices: beware of counterfeit currency.

Biennale

See (events) p. 101

Camp sites (Campeggi)

Peninsula Cavallino	There are camp sites with good facilities on the Cavallino Peninsula (opposite the northern tip of the Lido). Access by car: via Jésolo. Motor launch: Treporti–Burano–Venice.
Lido	"Adriatico" camp site, Via Sandro Gallo, 215. Car ferry and motor launches.
Mestre	"Venezia" camp site (4 km/2½ miles) E of Mestre.
Ca'Noghera	"Alba d'Oro" camp site (near the airport).

Chemists (Farmacie)

Opening times	Summer: 8.30 a.m.–12.30 p.m., 4–8 p.m. Winter: 8.30 a.m.–12.30 p.m., 3.30–7.30 p.m.
Farmacia di turno	Chemists that take it in turns to provide a service at night, on Sundays and public holidays are listed in the local paper "Il Gazzettino" under "Farmacia di turno".

Climate

Air temperature: December–February +6 °C (42 °F); March/April and October/November about 17 °C (62 °F); May–September 21–27 °C (69–80 °F).
Sustained periods of bad weather are usually in the early spring and Venice is occasionally blasted by that hot wind from the south, the Sirocco, in the summer months.
Sea Temperature: April 14 °C (57 °F); July 26 °C (79 °F); October 17 °C (62 °F).

Consulate

Great Britain	P.O. Box 679 (Callers: Accademia 1051; tel. 27 207).

Currency

Currency	The unit of currency is the *lira* (plural *lire*). There are banknotes for 500, 1,000, 2,000, 5,000, 10,000, 50,000, and 100,000 lire and coins in the denominations of 5, 10, 20, 50, 100, 200 and 500 lire. The 500 lire banknote is being withdrawn. There is often a shortage of small coins, and telephone tokens (*gettoni*) or postage stamps may be used to make up the deficiency.

There are no restrictions on the import of foreign currency into Italy, but in view of the strict controls on the export of currency it is advisable to declare any currency brought in on the appropriate form (modulo V£) at the frontier.
There is a limit of 400,000 lire per head on the import of Italian currency.

Import of currency

The export of foreign currency is permitted only up to a value of 1 million lire per person except where a larger sum has been declared on entry. No more than 400,000 lire of Italian currency can be taken out.

Export of currency

It is advisable to take money in the form of travellers' cheques, which are not subject to any restrictions, or to use a Euro bank card. The principal credit cards are widely accepted.

Travellers' cheques, etc.

See under Banks.

Changing money

Customs regulations

Visitors to Italy can take in, without liability to duty, normal articles for personal use; visitors over 15 years of age can take in 1,000 g coffee or 400 g powdered coffee and 200 g tea or 80 g tea extract, and for visitors over 17 years of age $1\frac{1}{2}$ litres spirits over 22% or 3 litres spirits below 22% or 3 litres sparkling wine and 5 litres wine, as well as 300 cigarettes or 74 cigars or 400 g of tobacco. Visitors over 15 years of age may import in addition goods and presents up to a total value of 490,000 lire. Video apparatus must be declared on entry. The import of weapons – real or imitation – and sheath and multi-purpose knives is forbidden.

Entry

Visitors can take out, without liability to duty, articles they have bought in Italy up to the value of 500 US dollars. For the export of objets d'art and antiques a permit must be obtained from the Chamber of Art.

Departure

If large sums of cash are taken in to Italy it is advisable in every case to make a declaration on entry (see Currency).

Note

Events

The programme of events is published in the daily paper "Il Gazzettino" under local news and can also be obtained from tourist offices.

"Carnevale", Venetian carnival.

February

"Vogalonga" boat-race.

May

Biennale d'Arte. Biennial art exhibition until September (1984, etc.).

June

Third Sunday in July: Festa del Redentore (Festival of the Redeemer) commemorating the end of the plague in 1576, culminating in an illuminated procession of gondolas and other craft on the Canale della Giudecca with music and fireworks (see Venice A–Z, La Giudecca).

July

Film festival (until September).

August

Practical Information

September	First Sunday: Regatta storica. Historical gondola regatta on the Canal Grande.
November	21 November: Festa della Madonna della Salute, to commemorate the end of the plague in 1630. A large procession of pilgrims makes its way from the Basilica di San Marco (see Venice A–Z) over a bridge of boats on the Canal Grande to the Church of Santa Maria della Salute (see Venice A–Z).

Excursions

Lido	See Venice A–Z, Lido.
Punta Sabbioni/ Lido di Jésolo	From the Lido there is a motor-boat service (and also a car ferry) to Punta Sabbioni from which a road runs 20 km (12½ miles) NE to the large resort of Lido di Jésolo which, with its beautiful broad beach, ranks with Rimini, Riccioni and the Venice Lido as one of the most popular resorts on the Adriatic.
Murano	See Venice A–Z, Murano.
Burano	See Venice A–Z, Burano.
Torcello	See Venice A–Z, Torcello.
Chioggia	By boat (from the Riva Schiavoni) and bus it takes 1½ hours to get to the interesting island town of Chioggia near the S end of the lagoon. Formerly the centre of the Venetian salt production and destroyed by the Genoese in 1379, it is now Italy's largest fishing port. Sights: Cathedral, Church of San Martino. A bridge 800 m (875 yd) long leads from the old town of Chioggia to Sottomarina, a popular bathing resort with a good beach.
Where to book	Excursions to places in the vicinity of Venice can be booked in most travel agencies and hotels.

First aid (Pronto soccorso)

Emergency service	Anywhere in Italy you can dial 113 for ambulance, fire or police.
Blue Cross	Pronto Soccorso Autoambulanze. Venice: tel. 30 000. Mestre: tel. 98 89 88.
Red Cross (Croce Rosso)	Posto Pronto Soccorso. Venice: tel. 86 346. San Marco 52. Mestre: tel. 95 09 88.
Casualty departments (Pronto Soccorso Accettaziono Ammalati)	Ospedale al Mare; tel. 76 17 50 (Lungomare d'Annunzio, 1, Lido). Ospedale Gen. Prov. le Mestre; tel. 98 89 88.

Blood transfusions (Pronto soccorso e trasfusioni di sangue), tel. 76 87 00 (Lido).

Blood transfusions

By motor-launch ambulance (Venice–Lido); tel. 76 87 00.

See (chemists) p. 100.

Chemists

See (hospitals) p. 107.

Hospitals

Food and drink

The food served in hotels is mainly international with an Italian emphasis.

Food and drink

The menu is usually in Italian but the waiter will be glad to help with explanations and will be able to recommend local specialities. Hotel breakfasts are of the kind found throughout most of Europe. Italians themselves do not have breakfast as we know it.

Luncheon (pranzo or colzione) is usually served between noon and 3 p.m. and dinner (cena) between 8 and 10 p.m.

Venetian cuisine is largely dominated by local seafood – shrimps, squid, shellfish and fish from the lagoon.

Some Venetian specialities:

Brodetto di pesce: soup of fish from the Adriatic with onions, tomato juice, white wine, parsley, bay leaves and oil.
Broèto: eel soup.
Risi e luganega: rice soup with pork sausages.

Soups (Minestre)

Cannelloni ripieni: tubular pieces of pasta filled with meat in a tomato sauce.
Gnocchi alla Fontina: semolina dumplings with grated Fontina cheese.
Gnocchi di patate: potato dumplings with a cheese sauce.
Pappardelle con funghi: long noodles with mushrooms.
Risi e bisi: rice with fresh peas and ham (the staple Venetian dish).
Risotto de peoci o de cape: rice with shellfish, crabs, shrimps, etc.
Soppressa: Venetian sausage.
Spaghetti con vongole: spaghetti with shellfish.

Hors d'œuvres
(Antipasta)

Castradina alla griglia: grilled lamb.
Fegato alla veneziana: calf's liver thinly sliced and cooked in butter with onions.

Meat dishes

Anguille alla veneziana: eel cooked in a sauce of lemon and tunny.
Asia bolito: boiled whitefish.
Baccala alla vicenta: salt cod simmered in milk.
Coda di rospo al ferri: grilled anglerfish.
Calamari fritti: squid rings fried in batter.
Dorate: a fish from the Adriatic.
Filetti di San Pietro fritti: fillets of St Peter's fish, coated in egg and flour and fried.
Go: fish from the Venetian lagoon.

Fish dishes

Mansanete: fried crabs.
Moleche: soft-shelled crayfish.
Orate al ferri: grilled gilt-head bream.
Seppie ai ferri con polenta: grilled small squid with maize flour cakes.
Sogliola alla casserualo: casseroled sole with mushrooms.
Triglie con risi: sea perch with rice.

Tipping

The usual tip in restaurants is 5–10% of the bill. Service is not included in the bill in Italian cafés and bars so it is usual to tip 12–15% even when sitting at the bar.

Wine

Italians usually drink wine, especially local wines, with their meals, almost always accompanied by mineral water.

Local white wines from Veneto include –
Very dry (asciutto): Breganze bianco, Prosecco.
Dry (secco): Bianco di Conliano, Gambellara.
Fruity (abboccato): Barbarano bianco, Tokai, Verdiso.
Medium dry: Soave.
Sweet: Recioto.

Sweet dessert wines: Moscato di Arqua, Prosecco Spumante.

Local red wines from Veneto include –
Very dry (asciutto): Barbarano rosso, Breganze rosse Cabernet di Treviso, Friularo.
Dry (secco): Bardolino, Merlot, Ricioto Amarone, Valpantena, Valpolicella.
Fruity (abboccato): Redioto rosso, Rubino della Marca, Rubino del Piave.

Restaurants

See (restaurants) p. 120.

Food Shops (Alimentari)

Although more and more supermarkets are opening up, Venetians still prefer to buy their cheese, ham, sausages, tinned foodstuffs and pasta daily in the small corner shop, the "Alimentari" or "Salumeria", which usually also sells bread and slices of pizza.

Panificio

Bread (mainly white) is usually bought in the "Panificio".

Pasticceria

Shops that make and sell cakes and pastries.

Opening times

Summer: Mon.–Fri. 9 a.m.–1 p.m. and 4–8 p.m. Sat. 9 a.m.– 1 p.m.
Winter: Mon.–Fri. 8 a.m.–1 p.m. and 3.30–7.30 p.m.
Closed: Mon. afternoons.

Weight

In kilos and grams, apart from 1 etto=100 grams.

Galleries

Galleria dell'Accademia.
See Venice A–Z, Galleria dell'Accademia.

Galleria d'Arte Orientale.
See Venice A–Z, Palazzo Pesaro.

Galleria Franchetti – Ca'd'Oro.
See Venice A–Z, Ca'd'Oro.

Galleria Internazionale d'Arte Moderna.
See Venice A–Z, Palazzo Pesaro.

Pinacoteca Manfrediniana.
See Venice A–Z, Seminario e Pinacoteca Manfrediania.

Pinacoteca di Pallazo Ducale.
See Venice A–Z, Palazzo Ducale (Doges' Palace).

Pinacoteca Querini-Stampalia.
See Venice A–Z, Palazzo Querini-Stampalia.

Raccolta Peggy Guggenheim.
See Venice A–Z, Ca'Venier dei Leoni.

See (Museums) page 112.   Museums

Getting to Venice

Since 1933 the island city of Venice has been joined to the   By car
mainland by a roadbridge (3·6 km/2 miles), thus connecting
Venice with the European motorway system via the autostrada
from Milan to Trieste.

The roadbridge, the Ponte della Liberta, brings drivers into   Parking
Venice where they can park on the island of Tronchetto
(signposted: per Tronchetto) and near the Piazzale Roma in a
multi-storey car park (Autorimessa Comunale) where there is
also an accommodation bureau. In addition there are on the
mainland to the N and S of the road bridge, two further official
car parks: San Giuliano (motor boat 24 to the town) and Fusina
(motor boat 16 to the town). It is advisable, if coming from
Jésolo, to leave the car at Punta Sabbioni and continue by boat
or, if coming from the mainland, to park in Mestre or Marghera
and then take the railway or the coach.

Tolls are payable on most Italian motorways (autostrada). A   Motorways
travel ticket is issued on entry and the toll is paid on leaving the
motorway.

Motorists should carry their driving licence and car registration   Documents, etc.
document. An international insurance certificate ("green
card") is not obligatory but is advisable. The car should have a
nationality plate, and a warning triangle must be carried.

There is a wide choice of routes from the Channel Ports to   Roads to Venice
Venice depending on individual preferences and time available
– through France and over one of the Alpine passes into Italy;
down to the S coast of France and then on the coastal
motorway into Italy; by France or Germany, Switzerland and
one of the Alpine passes or tunnels. The journey can be
shortened by using one of the motorail services from stations in
NW Europe.

Practical Information

Frontier crossings

Switzerland–Italy.
The major frontier crossings open round the clock between Switzerland and Italy –

Simplon Tunnel: Brig–Iselle–Milan.
Chiasso: Lugano–Como–Milan.
Castesegna/Chiavenna (Maloya Pass): St Moritz–Milan.

Austria–Italy
The following frontier crossings between Austria and Italy are open round the clock –

Brenner Pass: Innsbruck–Bolzano.
Reschen Pass: Landeck–Merano–Bolzano.
Winnbach (Prato alle Drava): Lienz–Venice.
Tarvisio: Villach–Udine–Venice.

By coach

There are numerous package tours by coach either going direct to Venice or including Venice on a longer circuit. For information apply to any travel agent.
There are also various coach services between Britain or northern Europe and Venice. Euroways run a regular service from London via Milan to Venice.

By air

There are daily scheduled flights from London to Venice and weekly flights from Manchester to Venice.
Marco Polo International Airport (Aeroporto Internazionale) lies near Téssara. Buses run into Venice as far as the Air Terminal (Aerostazione). Fondamenta di Son Chiara near the Piazzale Roma (Canal Grande). There is a motor-boat service (motoscafi) to San Marco which takes 30 minutes.
Private flights land at Nicelli Airport (Aeroporto Nicelli) at San Nicolò di Lido (Lido). There is a motor-boat service from San Nicolò to Riva degli Schiavoni (near San Marco).

Airlines

See page 99.

By sea

There are connections to all the major Adriatic ports as well as to Rhodes and Piraeus. Venice is a favourite port of embarkation for cruises.
Cruise ships usually berth at Zattere or Riva degli Schiavoni. Information can be obtained from travel agencies or the Italian State Travel Office (see (Tourist Information) p. 123).

By rail

The fastest route from London to Venice takes just over 25 hours leaving London (Charing Cross) at 9 am, crossing the Channel by Hovercraft and changing in Paris. Twice a week the legendary Orient Express (restored) travels from London via Paris and Lausanne to Venice.

Arrival in Venice
Since 1846 Venice has been linked to the mainland by a railway bridge that connects its terminal, Santa Lucia Station, with the international rail network. (Accommodation reservations can also be made at the station.)

Hospitals (Ospedali)

Ospedale Civile:
Venice, Fondamenta dei Medicanti/Campo dei SS Giovanni e
Paolo; tel. 70 56 22.
Motor boat: 5 (to Fondamenta Nuove).

Ospedale Civile:
Mestre, Via Circonvallazione 50; tel. 95 79 44, 98 12 00.

Ospedale al Mare:
Lido di Venezia, Lungomare d'Annunzio 1; tel. 76 01 80,
76 06 28, 76 11 40, 76 14 13, 76 17 01.
Motor boat: 1, 2, 3, 4, 5, 6, 17.

See (first aid) page 102.   First aid

See (insurance) page 109.   Health insurance

Hotels (Alberghi)

Hotels are officially classified in five categories, from luxury   Categories
(5 stars) to hotels or pensions with modest amenities (1 star).

Tariffs vary considerably according to season. The rates given   Tariffs
in the following table (in lire) are based on information given
in the Italian State Tourist Office's list of hotels "Alberghi
d'Italia". Increases can be expected. Hotel bills should be kept
in case of inquiry by Government Inspectors into possible tax
evasion.

N.B. Receipted bills for accommodation and meals, etc. in
Italian establishments must be retained and shown to a tax
inspector on demand. Failure to do so entails a fine.

Category	Single room Rate for 1 person	Double room Rate for 2 persons
*****	140,000–350,000	200,000–500,000
****	65,000–140,000	100,000–200,000
***	35,000– 65,000	50,000–100,000
**	25,000– 40,000	35,000– 60,000
*	15,000– 30,000	25,000– 40,000

In the centre
*****

Bauer Grunwald & Grand Hotel, Campo San Moise 1459, tel.
70 70 22, 214 r.
Cipriani, Giudecca 10, tel. 70 77 44, 98 r.
Danieli, Riva degli Schiavoni 4196, tel. 2 64 80, 239 r.
Europa & Regina, San Marco 2159, tel. 70 04 77, 200 r.
Gritti Palace, Campo Santa Maria del Giglio 2467, tel. 79 46 11,
99 r.

Practical Information

****

Carlton Executive, Anta Croce 578, tel. 71 84 44, 130 r.
Cavalletto & Doge Orseolo, Calle del Cavalletto 1107, tel. 70 09 55, 80 r.
Etap Park Hotel, Giardini Papadopoli, tel. 8 53 94, 100 r.
Gabrielli-Sandwirth, Riva degli Schiavoni 4110, tel. 3 15 80, 111 r.
Londra Palace, Riva degli Schiavoni 4171, tel. 70 05 33, 69 r.
Luna, Calle Larga dell'Ascensione 1243, tel. 8 98 40, 125 r.
Metropole, Riva degli Schiavoni 4149, tel. 70 50 44, 64 r.
Monaco & Grand Canal, Calle Vallaresso 1325, tel. 70 02 11, 75 r.
Saturnia & International, Calle Larga 22 Marzo 2399, tel. 70 83 77, 99 r.
Splendid Suisse, San Marco-Mercerie 760, tel. 70 07 55, 155 r.

***

Bisanzio, Calle della Pieta, tel. 70 31 00, 39 r.
Bonvecchiati, Calle Goldoni 4488, tel. 8 50 1 7, 86 r.
Carpaccio, Calle Corner 2765, tel. 3 59 46, 17 r.
Concordia, Calle Larga San Marco 367, tel. 70 68 66, 60 r.
Continental, Lista di Spagna 166, tel. 71 51 22, 104 r.
Flora, Calle Larga 22 Marzo 2283/a, tel. 70 58 44, 44 r.
La Fenice et Des Artistes, Campiello de la Fenice 1936, tel. 3 23 33, 68 r.
Savoia & Jolanda, Riva degli Schiavoni 4187, tel. 70 66 44, 71 r.
San Marco, Calle dei Fabbri 877, tel. 70 42 77, 60 r.

**

Ateneo, San Marco 1876, tel. 70 05 88, 20 r.
Basilea, Rio Marin 817, tel. 71 84 77, 30 r.
La Residenza, Campo Bandiera e Moro 3608, tel. 8 53 15, 14 r.
Skandinavia, Santa Maria Formosa 5240, tel. 70 59 65, 31 r.

On the Lido
*****

Excelsior, Lungomare Marconi 41, tel. 76 02 01, 220 r.

****

Des Bains, Lungomare Marconi 17, tel. 76 59 21, 266 r.
Quattro Fontane, Via 4 Fontane 16, tel. 76 08 14, 70 r.
Villa Mabapa, Riviera S. Nicolo 16, tel. 76 05 90, 63 r.

***

Adria Urania – Villa Nora & Ada, Viale Dandolo 29, tel. 76 01 20, 85 r.
Helvetia, Gran Viale S. M. Elisabetta 4, tel. 76 01 05, 50 r.
Petit Palais, Lungomare Marconi 54, tel. 76 59 93, 25 r.
Rigel, Viale Dandolo 13, tel. 76 01 58, 42 r.
Villa Otello, Via Lepanto 12, tel. 76 00 48, 34 r.

In Mestre
****

Ambasciatori, Corso del Popolo 221, tel. 5 31 06 99, 104 r.
Michelangelo, Via Forte Marghera 69, tel. 98 66 00, 51 r.
Motel Agip, loc. Marghera, tel. 93 69 00, 188 r.

***

Bologna & Stazione, Via Piave 214, tel. 93 10 00, 130 r.
Lugano Torretta, loc. Marghera, tel. 93 67 77, 62 r.
Mondial, loc. Marghera, tel. 93 01 67, 66 r.
Plaza, Piazzale Stazione 36, tel. 92 93 88, 226 r.
President, Via Forte Marghera 99/a, tel. 98 56 55, 51 r.

San Giuliano, Via Forte Marghera 193 A, tel. 95 76 04, 58 r.   **
Venezia, Piazza 27 Ottobre, tel. 98 55 33, 100 r.
Vivit, Piazza Ferretto 73, tel. 95 13 85, 19 r.

r=rooms.

You can freshen up, change, deposit your luggage, visit the   Daytime hotels
hairdresser or simply relax for a time in the so called "daytime"   (Alberghi Diurni)
hotels. In Venice these are to be found in San Marco, Calle dell'
Ascensione (W of the Piazza de San Marco) and in the main
railway station (Stazione Santa Lucia).

See Student hostels.   Student hostels

Insurance

It is very desirable to have an international insurance certificate   Car insurance
("green card"), although this is not a legal requirement for
citizens of EEC countries. It is important to have fully
comprehensive cover, and it is desirable to take out short-term
insurance against legal costs if these are not already covered.
Italian insurance companies tend to be slow in settling claims.

British visitors to Italy, like other EEC citizens, are entitled to   Health insurance
receive health care on the same basis as Italians (including free
medical treatment, etc.); they should apply to their local social
security office, well before their date of departure, for a
certificate of entitlement (Form E111). Fuller cover can be
obtained by taking out insurance against medical expenses;
and non-EEC citizens will, of course, be well advised to take out
appropriate insurance cover.

In view of the risk of theft it is desirable to have adequate   Baggage insurance
insurance against loss of, or damage to, baggage.

Libraries

Biblioteca Nazionale Marciana.
See Venice A–Z, Zecca and Libreria Vecchia
(exhibition rooms).

Collezione della Fondazione Giorgio Cini.
See Venice A–Z, San Giorgio Maggiore.
The collection of the Monastery of San Giorgio Maggiore can
only be seen by prior appointment.

Raccolte dei Padri Armeni Mechitaristi,
San Lazzaro degli Armeni (Island).
Open Mon.–Sat. 3–5 p.m.
Collection of pictures, books and manuscripts.

Pinacoteca Querini-Stampalia.
See Venice A–Z, Palazzo Querini-Stampalia.

Lost property offices (Servizi oggetti rinvenuti)

Municipal lost
property office

Riva del Carbon, Pallazo Farsetti (city hall), Campo San Luca.

Municipal
transport

The lost property office of ACNIL (city public transport): tel. 2
09 21.

Markets (Mercati)

Pescheria.
See Venice A–Z, Pescheria.

Erberia.
Canal Grande.
Boats unload fruit and vegetables here in the late afternoon.

Fruit market,
Campo Santa Maria Formosa.

Motoring

The road system

The main types of road are:
Motorways (*autostrade*), numbered A .... Tolls are payable.
State highways (*strade statali*), numbered SS .... Many of
them have names (Via Aurelia, Via Emilia, etc.), which are often
better known than their numbers.
Provincial highways (*strade di grande comunicazione*), which
have no numbers.
Secondary roads (*strade secondarie*), for local traffic.

Speed limits

Within built-up areas the speed limit is 50 km p.h. (31 m.p.h.).
Outside built-up areas the limits vary according to cylinder
capacity.

Capacity
up to 600 cc
up to 900 cc
up to 1300 cc
over 1300 cc

Ordinary roads	Motorways
80 km p.h. (50 m.p.h.)	90 km p.h. (56 m.p.h.)
90 km p.h. (56 m.p.h.)	110 km p.h. (68 m.p.h.)
100 km p.h. (62 m.p.h.)	130 km p.h. (81 m.p.h.)
110 km p.h. (68 m.p.h.)	140 km p.h. (87 m.p.h.)

Safety-belts

The wearing of safety-belts is strongly recommended.

Compulsory equipment

All motorists must carry a warning triangle and it is
recommended that visitors equip themselves with a spare set of
light bulbs.

Priority

Traffic on main roads has priority when the road is marked with
the priority sign – a square with a corner pointing downwards,
coloured white with a red border or yellow with a black and
white border.
At roundabouts traffic on the right has priority.

Mountain roads

On mountain roads traffic going up has priority.

Any change of lane (for overtaking or any other purpose) must be signalled with the direction indicator, as must an intention to stop by the roadside.	Change of lane
Outside built-up areas the horn must be sounded before overtaking. It must also be sounded before intersections, side roads, blind bends and other hazards. After dark flashing headlights should be used for the same purpose.	Overtaking
Children under 3 are not permitted to travel in a vehicle as front-seat passengers.	Passengers
In towns the use of the horn is frequently prohibited, either by an appropriate road sign (a horn with a stroke through it) or by the legend "Zona di silenzio".	Prohibition on use of horn
On well-lit roads only sidelights may be used (except in tunnels and galleries where dipped headlights must be used at all times).	Lights
Pedestrians have absolute priority on zebra crossings.	Zebra crossings
The directions of the traffic police (*polizia stradale*) should be exactly complied with. Fines for traffic offences are high.	Traffic police
There are heavy penalties for driving under the influence of drink.	Drink and driving
It is forbidden to carry petrol in cans in a vehicle. A package of petrol coupons giving a saving on the pump price can be purchased from the AA or at main ports and border crossings.	Petrol
In case of accident make sure that you have all the necessary particulars and supporting evidence (statements by witnesses, sketches, photographs, etc.). If the accident involves personal injury it must be reported to the police. You should notify your own insurance company as soon as possible, and if you are responsible or partly responsible for the accident you should also inform the Italian insurance company or bureau whose address is given on your "green card". This agency will give advice and supply the name of a lawyer should the foreign driver be subject to penal proceedings. – If your car is a total write-off the Italian Customs authorities must be informed at once, since otherwise you might be required to pay the full import duty on the vehicle.	Accidents
Automobile Club d'Italia (ACI). Venice branch office: Fondamenta Son Chiara, Piazzale Roma 518/a; tel. 70 03 00. Mestre branch office: Corso Popolo 131.	Automobile clubs
In case of breakdown on any Italian road just dial 116 at the nearest telephone box. Tell the operator where you are, your vehicle registration number and type of car, and the nearest ACI office will be informed for immediate assistance.	Breakdown service
Look for the sign "Riparazione Gomme".	Puncture repair
Look for "Officina".	Repair garages
Anywhere in Italy, dial 113.	Police and ambulance

Museums

Collezione Cini in Palazzo Cini, San Vio D.D. 864.
Open Tues.–Sun. 2–7 p.m.; closed Mon.

Collezione Peggy Guggenheim.
See A to Z, Ca'Venier dei Leoni e Raccolta Peggy Guggenheim.

Museo Archeologica.
See Venice A–Z, Museo Archeologico.

Museo d'Arte Vetraria (Glass Museum).
See Venice A–Z, Murano.

Casa Goldoni
in the Palazzo Centanni, Calle Nomboli 2793, near the Campo
San Polo.
Open Mon.–Sat. 8.30 a.m.–1.30 p.m., closed: Sun., public
holidays; birthplace of Goldoni, now Theatre Institute.

Museo Civico Correr with the Museo del Risorgimento.
See Venice A–Z, Museo Civico Correr e Museo del Risorgimento.

Museo Civico di Storia Naturale.
See Venice A–Z, Fondaco dei Turchi.

Museo della Comunità Israelitica (Jewish Museum).
See Venice A–Z, Il Ghetto.

Museo Diocesano (Diocesan Museum)
in the former monastery of Sant' Apollonia, Castello.
Castello 4912.
Open Mon.–Sat. 10.30 a.m.–12.30 p.m., closed Sun. and
public holidays.

Museo di Icone dell'Instituto Ellenico (Museum of Icons).
See Venice A–Z, Museo di Icone dell'Instituto Ellenico.

Museo Mariciano (Museum of San Marco).
See Venice A–Z, Basilica di San Marco.

Museo dell'Opera di Palazzo Ducale.
See Venice A–Z, Palazzo Ducale.

Museo di Palazzo Fortuny,
Campo San Beneto.
Open Tues.–Sun. 8.30 a.m.–1.30 p.m.; closed Mon.

Museo Provinciale,
Torcello.
Open Tues.–Sun. 10.30 a.m.–12.30 p.m., 2–4.30 p.m.
Closed Mon.

Museo del Settecento Veneziano.
See Venice A–Z, Pallazo Rezzonico.

Museo Storico Navale (Maritime Museum).
See Venice A–Z, Museo Storico Navale.

Music

Opera/ballet

Teatro La Fenice,
Campo San Fantin.
See Venice A–Z, Teatro La Fenice.

Conservatorio di Musica Benedetto Marcello, Santo Stefano 2810.

Concerts

Palazzo Labia, Fondamenta Labia. Motor boat: 1 (to San Marcuola). RAI, the Italian radio station, occasionally puts on concerts.

Musical performances

Musical gondola trips on the Canal Grande from May to September, departing at 9 p.m. from Bauer-Grünwald Hotel. Advance booking: CIT, Piazza San Marco.

Gondola serenades

Nightlife

Casino Municipale – From 31 March to 1 October in the Palazzo Vendramin-Calergi, Canal Grande. From 30 September to 1 April in the Palazzo del Casino, Lido. Open evenings all year round.

Casino

Motor launches: there are two motor launches (motoscafo diretto) as well as the motor-boat service between the Casino on the Lido and the main railway station, the Piazzale Roma (Fondameta San Chiara) and San Marco (Giardini).

The best known of these restaurants are: Antico Pignolo, Calle Specchieri 451; L'Arlecchino, Hotel Bauer Grünwald, San Moisè 1440; Night Club Antico Martini, San Marco 1880; Parco delle Rose, Lido; Gran Viale; Blue Moon, Lido, Piazzale Sergher.

Restaurants with night-time entertainment

Opening times

9 a.m.–1 p.m. and 3.30–7.30 p.m.; July–September: 9 a.m.– 1 p.m. and 4–8 p.m.

Shops

Closed: foodshops: Monday morning; other shops: Wednesday afternoon; hairdressers: Monday.

The public museums are generally open from 9 or 10 a.m. to 1 or 2 p.m. and from 2 or 3 to 5 or 6, rarely to 7 p.m.; a few remain open throughout the day, without a lunch break. In winter (when the museums are for the most part inadequately heated) the opening hours are usually shorter, but during the more restricted hours they often remain open without a break at lunchtime. All museums are closed on Sunday afternoons and statutory public holidays; most of them are also closed on Mondays or sometimes on Fridays. On various other days in the year the State museums are open only in the mornings and other museums are closed all day. In addition, there are often closures as a result of staff shortages, strikes, renovation, etc. It is advisable, therefore, before visiting a museum to check that it will be open.

Museums

The larger churches are usually open until 12 noon and for the most part also from 4 or 5 p.m. until dusk; some of the major churches are open all day. It is possible to see the interior of a

Churches

church during a service if care is taken to avoid disturbing the worshippers. Visitors should always be suitably dressed, avoiding sleeveless dresses or blouses, miniskirts, shorts, short-sleeved shirts, etc. If inappropriately dressed they may be refused admittance; cover-up garments can be hired at the entrance of some churches.

During Lent almost all altar pieces are covered and not shown to visitors.

Palaces (Palazzi)

Venice has more than 900 palaces. Although totally different in style, furnishings, and size they have one thing in common: every palace has one main façade, overlooking either a canal or a campo; the other three sides are uninteresting, plain and often almost shabby. This applies particularly to the palaces on the Canal Grande which means there is no point in looking for the street entrance to a palace unless it houses a museum or a gallery.

For all the other palaces (and that is about 80% of them) it is enough just to look at their principal façade from a boat on one of the canals.

A good way to gain at least a first impression of the imposing façades on both sides of the Canal Grande is to take Line 1, the boat service that plies the whole length of the Canal Grande, with stopping-off points at frequent intervals (see (sightseeing tours), p. 121).

Pets

In view of the stringent regulations regarding the prevention of rabies you are strongly advised not to attempt to take pets out of the UK or to bring them in when you return.

Police (Carabiniere)

Questura	Police Headquarters. Passport and Aliens Department; tel. 70 32 22.
Flying Squad	Venice: tel. 360 00. Mestre: tel. 577 77.
Polizia Stradale	Traffic police, Mestre, Via Ca' Rossa 14; tel. 96 17 22, 5 61 11.
Vigili Urbani	Municipal police: Palazzo Loredan; tel. 240 63. Piazzale Roma; tel. 2 21 62, 245 76. Lido: Via Sandro Gallo; tel. 76 03 95. Mestre: Via Slongo 22; tel. 561 03.
Carabinieri	Emergency service (pronto intervento): Venice: San Zaccaria; tel. 322 22. Mestre: tel 5 55 55.

Postal services

Letters within Italy and to EEC countries 500 lire; postcards 450 lire.

Postal rates

Stamps can be bought at post offices, at tobacconists' (indicated by a large T above the door) and from stamp machines.

Stamps (francobolli)

Palazzo Fondaco dei Tedeschi (near the Ponte di Rialto). This is the only post office that can be used for poste restante.
Open Mon.–Sat. 9 a.m.–8 p.m., Sun. 9 a.m.–noon.

Head Post Office (Posta centrale) and telegraph office

Ufficio Principale Telegrafico Centrale (Head Post Office).
Stazione Santa Lucia (main railway station).
Poste e Telegrafi, Calle dell'Ascensione.
Open Mon.–Fri. 8.15 a.m.–2 p.m.
Telegrams by telephone: tel. 850 72.

Telegrams (day and night)

Public holidays

1 January (New Year's Day); Easter; 25 April (Liberation Day, 1945); 1 May (Labour Day); 1st Sunday in June (Proclamation of the Republic); 15 August (Assumption: a family celebration, the high point of the Italian summer holiday migration); 1 November (All Saints); 1st Sunday in November (Day of National Unity); 8 December (Immaculate Conception); 25 and 26 December (Christmas).

Public transport

Vaporetti (canal steamers), motoscafi (motor launches) and motonavi (motor boats) provide Venice with its public transport, operating between the different parts of the city and also connecting the city with the islands.

They run between 5 a.m. and 10.45 p.m. or later.

The fares depend on the length of the journey and on the time of day.

A free map giving information on all public transport can be obtained from the information offices (see (Tourist Information) page 123).

The Canal Grande is the most important route for traffic in the Canal Grande Venice. The boat-stops on the Canal Grande are as follows:

No. 1: Piazzale Roma
No. 2: Ferrovia (Main railway station)
No. 3: Riva Biasio

No. 4: San Marcuola
No. 5: San Staè
No. 6: Ca' d'Oro
No. 7: Rialto
No. 8: San Silvestro
No. 9: San Angelo
No. 10: San Tomà (Frari Church)
No. 11: Ca' Rezzonico
No. 12: Accademia
No. 13: Santa Maria del Giglio (Fenice)
No. 14: Salute
No. 15: San Marco
No. 16: San Zaccaria
No. 17: Arsenale
No. 18: Giardini (-Esposizione)
No. 19: Santa Elena
No. 20: Lido

Lagoon

Route 1 (Vaporetto): Piazzale Roma–Canal Grande–Lido and back. Time taken: about 1 hour. Departure every 10 minutes calling at every stop.

Route 2 (Diretto): Express service along the Canal Grande to the Lido.
Rialto–Ferrovia–Piazzale Roma–San Samule–Accademia–San Marco–San Zaccaria–Santa Elena–Lido and return.
Time taken: about 40 minutes. Departure: every 10 minutes.

Route 3 (Directissimo): from the Tronchetto car park through the Canale della Giudecca to San Zaccaria (without stopping) – Lido and back.
Time taken: about 30 minutes. Departure: every 15 minutes.

Route 4 (Diretto): Piazzale Roma–Ferrovia–Rialto–San Tomà–Accademia–San Marco–San Zaccaria–Lido and back.
Time taken: about 45 minutes. Departure: every 20 minutes.

Route 5 (Circolare): circular route in both directions; Riva degli Schiavoni–Celestia–Fondamenta Nuove–Isola San Michele–Murano; or in a westerly direction via Piazzale Roma.
Time taken: 1 hour 45 minutes. Departure: every 15 minutes.

Route 6: Direct line between Venice and Lido.
Time taken: 15 minutes. Departure: from the Riva degli Schiavoni (Doges' Palace) every 20 minutes.

Route 9 (Traghetto): Ferry from Zattere to Giudecca and back.
Departure: every 15 minutes.

Route 11: Venice–Chioggia (by boat and bus).
Time taken: 1 hour 30 minutes.
Departure: Riva degli Schiavoni (Doges' Palace).

Route 12: Fondamenta Nuove–Murano–Burano–Torcello. Modonna dell'Orto–San Alvise–Ponte Tre Archi–Zattere–Giudecca (St Eufemia Redentore–Ostello)–San Giorgio–Riva degli Schiavoni.
Time taken: 1 hour 10 minutes. Departure: Fondamenta Nuove.

Route 14. Connection to Jésolo (by bus from Punta Sabbioni).
Time taken: 45 minutes. Departure: from Riva degli Schiavoni.

In summer only

Route 15: express line to Jésolo.
Time taken: 25 minutes. Departure: from Riva degli Schiavoni, every hour.

Route 28: Express line to Venice Casino on the Lido.
Time taken: 25 minutes. Departure: Ferovia (railway station)
every 30 minutes from 5 p.m. to 2 a.m.

Route 17: from the Piazzale Roma/Tronchetto to the Lido (San   Car ferry
Nicolò) and Punta Sabbioni.
Time taken: 1 hour 25 minutes. Departure: three times a day
during the summer.

Main landing-stages: by the railway station and on the Molo,   Gondolas
in front of the Piazzetta.
Gondolas are usually hired by the hour. There is an extra charge
for luggage.

The motor launches can be hired for a tour of the city or for trips   Boat hire
round the lagoon. There is also an extra charge for luggage.   (motoscafi di nolo)

These also operate a regular service from the railway station or
the Piazzale Roma to the Ponte di Rialto and to the hotels round
San Marco and on the Lido.

Buses provide transport between Venice and the mainland.   Buses
For example buses leave from Piazzale Roma for Carpento (No.
2), Favora (No. 4), Mestre (No. 5) and Treviso (No. 8).
On the Lido buses operate between the landing-stages at San
Niccolò and Santa Maria Elisabetta and Lungomare Marconi
(Route A) and between Santa Maria Elisabetta and the public
beaches and Citta Giordano (Route B) or alternatively Alberoni
(Route C).
There is also a route conecting Santa Maria Elisabetta with
Alberoni, San Pietro in Volta and Pellestrina (Route 11).

Radio

Information on BBC overseas radio transmissions in English   Programmes in English
may be obtained from BBC External Services, P.O. Box 76,
Bush House, London WC2B 4PH.

The Italian Radio Service (RAI) broadcasts in the holiday
season various programmes for foreign tourists (news,
commentaries, etc.) in various languages including English.

The first national programme of the radio service (RAI; medium   Travel information
wave and VHF) broadcasts daily at 1.56 p.m. travel informa-
tion, also in English.

Radio Uno O.M. (medium wave) transmits daily at 1.55 p.m.
the programme Onda Verte in four languages (travel information and road conditions).

Further information can be obtained from the motoring
organisation or the police.

Rail services

The Italian railway system has a total length of 16,000 km   Ferrovie dello
(10,000 miles). Most of it is run by the Italian State Railways   Stato (FS)
(Ferrovie dello Stato; FS).
Information about rail services can be obtained from the Italian
State Tourist Office or from Italian State Railways offices
abroad:

Practical Information

United Kingdom	10 Charles II Street, London SW1; tel. (01) 434 3844.
United States of America	765 Route 83, Suite 105, Chicago, Ill. 5670 Wilshire Boulevard, Los Angeles, Cal. 668 Fifth Avenue, New York, NY.
Canada	2055 Peel Street, Suite 102, Montreal. 111 Richmond Street West, Suite 419, Toronto.
	In Italy there are Italian State Railways offices in towns throughout the country.
In Venice	Their office in Venice is: 48 Piazza San Marco (in the arcade near the Campanile) Open Mon.–Fri. 8.30 a.m.–12.30 p.m., 3–6.30 p.m. Sat. 8.30 a.m.–12.30 p.m. Closed Sun., public holidays.
Tickets	The validity of tickets on Italian Railways depends on the length of the journey, from 1 day (up to 250 km/155 miles) to 6 days (over 1,000 km/620 miles).
Children's Fare	Children under 4 accompanied by an adult travel free. Children from 4 to 14 travel at half fare.
Tourist Ticket	The Tourist Ticket (BTLC) permits any number of journeys in first or second class on the entire Italian network within a validity of 8, 15, 21 or 30 days.

Restaurants

*Antico Martini, San Marco, Campo San Fantin 1980.
*Harry's Bar, San Marco, Calle de Ca' Vallaresso 1323.
Taverna La Fenice, San Marco, Campiello della Fenice 1938.
La Caravella, Via 22 Marzo 2397.
Alla Colomba, San Marco, Piscine Frezzeria 1665.
Do Forni, San Marco 468/470.
Do Leoni, Riva degli Schiavoni 4175.
Antica Carbonera, San Marco, Calle Bembo 4648.
Al Colombo, San Marco, Campiello del Teatro Goldini 4619.
Al Campiello, Calle dei Fuseri 4346.
Montin, Dorsoduro, Fondamente Eremite 1147.
Al Giglio, Campo San Maria del Giglio 2477; and others.

Because prices for à la carte meals tend to be rather high, the "menu turistico", which is usually very good, is recommended. Also there are in addition to expensive "ristorante" many modest, but generally excellent, establishments called "Tavola calda", "Rosticceria" or "Fiaschetteria".

Rosticceria San Bartolomeo, Campo San Bartolomeo.
Lanterna da Tiziano, Campo San Luca.
Fiaschetteria Toscana.

N.B. Every restaurant must provide the customer with a receipted bill, which must be shown on demand to a Government inspector investigating tax evasion in the vicinity of the establishment. Failure to do so entails a fine.

Food and drink	See page 103.

Shopping

There are interesting shops in the arcades on the Piazza di San Marco, in the shopping street, the Merceria (see Venice A–Z, Merceria), around the Ponte di Rialto and in the Frezzeria behind the Piazza di San Marco (second steet over from the Ala Napoleonica). Good buys can be found in leather goods, textiles, articles in gold, silver and glass, as well as Venetian lace (especially lace embroidery from Burano).

Sightseeing

Check with the travel agencies (see page 123) that organise guided tours or with the tourist offices (see page 123)

City tours

A sightseeing tour Venetian style is a boat trip along the Canal Grande from the railway station to the Piazza di San Marco. You can choose between taking it easy on the "slow boat" (Vaporetto No. 1), calling at every stopping-place and the Diretto No. 2 which only stops at a few places.

Canal tours

The travel agencies offer a number of tours by boat (e.g. to the villas at Brenta) which take a whole day.
Information can be obtained from the travel agencies (see Travel agencies page 123) or from the tourist offices (see Tourist Information page 123).

Boat tours

These are also arranged by the travel agencies (see (Travel agencies) page 123).

Tours of the lagoon

An exclusive (hence expensive) way of visiting one of the islands is to hire a gondola for the trip, but it can happen that the hard-headed gondolier – "time is money" – hitches a lift from a motor boat and the journey is taken at a breakneck speed instead of the more romantic pace one had bargained for.

Gondolas

Student hostels

Casa della Studente Domus Civica,
San Rocco 3082.

Foresteria Maschile del Seminario C,
Santa Maria della Salute.
Open June–September.

Foresteria Renier Michiel,
San Trovaso 1134.
Open June–September.

Foresteria Universitaria di Ca' Foscari,
Dorsoduro 3861.

Taxis

Water taxis (taxi) ply along the Canal Grande.

Telephone

International dialling code from Venice	To the United Kingdom 00 44. (Direct dialling not available to the United States and Canada.)

International dialling codes to Venice

From the United Kingdom 010 39 41.
From the United States 011 39 41.
From Canada 011 39 41.

In dialling an international call the initial zero of the local dialling code should be omitted.

International calls

The best place to make international calls is the main post office (Officio Telefonico), Palazzo Fondaco dei Tedeschi (near the Ponte di Rialto) which is open for foreign language calls from 7 a.m. to 1 p.m. Long-distance calls can also be made at any of the other post offices which are open Monday to Friday from 8.15 a.m. to 2 p.m.

Public telephones

Telephone tokens (*gettoni*) as well as 100 and 200 lire coins can be used in public telephones. In addition most bars have public telephones (indicated by a yellow disc above the entrance to the box), operated by tokens (*gettoni*), from which local calls can be dialled. If the yellow disc bears the legend "teleselezione" or "interurbana" international calls can be dialled – though for this purpose you must provide yourself with an adequate supply of tokens.
A cheaper tariff operates daily between 10 p.m. and 8 a.m., as well as on Sundays and public holidays and on Saturdays and the eve of public holidays.

Theatres

Teatro la Fenice,
San Fantin 2549; tel. 2 51 91.

Teatro del Ridotto,
Calle Ca' Vallaresso, San Marco; tel. 2 29 39.

Teatro di Palazzo Grassi,
San Samuele 3231; tel. 2 46 00.

Teatro a l'Avorgaria,
Dorsoduro 1617; tel. 70 61 30.

Teatro Goldoni,
Calle Goldoni; tel. 70 58 38.

Time

Italy observes Central European Time (one hour ahead of Greenwich Mean Time; six hours ahead of New York time). From the beginning of April to the end of September summer time (two hours ahead of GMT; seven hours ahead of New York time) is in force.

Tipping (Mancia)

The usual tip in restaurants is 5–10% of the bill. Service is not included in the bill in Italian cafés and bars so it is usual to tip 12–15% even when sitting up at the bar.

Hotels/restaurants

Hairdressers expect 1,000–2,000 lire.

Hairdressers

The usual tip is 500 lire.

Porters

Tourist Information

The first place to go for information when you are planning a trip to Venice is the Italian State Tourist Office. Addresses:

1 Princes Street, London W1A 7RA; tel. (01) 408 1254.

United Kingdom

500 North Michigan Avenue, Chicago, IL 60611; tel. (312) 644 0990 1.
630 Fifth Avenue, Suite 1565, New York NY 10111; tel. (212) 245 4822–4.
360 Post Street, Suite 801, San Francisco, CA 94109; tel. (415) 392 6207.

United States of America

Store 56, Plaza, 3 Place Ville Maria, Montreal, Quebec; tel. (514) 866 7667.

Canada

Azienda Autonoma di Soggiorno e Turismo,
San Marco 4089; tel. 261 10.
Uffico Comune Turismo; tel. 70 07 92.
Ente Provinciale per il Turismo,
Castello 4421; tel. 2 23 73.

In Venice

Uffici Informazioni E.P.T.E.A.A.S.T.,
San Marco Ascensione 71/C; tel. 263 56.
Piazzale Roma, Stazione autolinee; tel. 274 02.
Lido, Gran Vitale; tel. 76 57 21.

Uffici Informazioni F.S.,
Stazione Santa Lucia (main railway station); tel. 715 555.

Italian Automobile Club (A.C.I.)
Fondamente San Chiara, Piazzale Roma 518/a; tel. 70 03 00.

Throughout Italy by dialling 116 information and advice can be obtained at any time (multi-lingual operators).

Information by telephone

Travel agencies (Uffici di viaggio)

ACI Tour Veneto,
Piazzale Roma 540; tel. 70 88 28.

American Express;
Main office: San Marco 1474 (near San Moisè); tel. 70 08 44.
Open Mon.–Fri. 8.45 a.m.–5 p.m.; Sat. 8.45 a.m.–12.30 p.m.
Branch office: Piazzale Roma (Autorimessa).

C.I.T. (Compagnia Italiana Turismo):
Main office: San Marco 4850 (Procuratie Nuove, near the Campanile); tel. 854 80.
Branch office: Piazzale Roma.

Guetta Travel Office
San Marco 1289; tel. 70 87 11.
Open Mon.–Fri. 9 a.m.–12.30 p.m.; 3–6.30 p.m.

Ital Travel
San Marco, Ascensione 72/B (at the end of the Procuratie Nuove); tel. 291 11.

Marco Polo,
Castello 4682/B (opposite church of San Zaccaria); tel. 352 28.

Romeatour,
Cannaregio 134; tel. 71 54 11.

Wagons Lits/Cook,
San Marco 289 (near the clock tower); tel. 234 05.

Travel documents

Passport

British and US citizens require only a passport (or the simpler British Visitor's Passport). This applies also to citizens of Canada, Ireland and many other countries.
If you lose your passport a substitute document can be issued by the British, US, Canadian, etc. consulate. It is a good idea to photocopy or note down the main particulars (number, date, etc.) of your passport, so that in case of loss you can give the necessary details to the police.

Driving licences, etc.

British, US and other national driving licences are valid in Italy, but must be accompanied by an Italian translation (obtainable free of charge from the AA). Motorists should also take the registration document of their car.

Green card

It is advisable (though not essential for EEC nationals) to have an international insurance certificate ("green card") if you are driving your own car.

Nationality plate

Foreign cars must display the oval nationality plate.

Youth hostels (Alberghi della Gioventù)

Ostello Venezia, Albergo della Gioventù,
Fondamenta Zitelle 86 (Isola della Giudecca); tel. 382 11.
Open: 1 March–31 October.

Student hostels

See Student hostels.

Useful Telephone Numbers at a Glance

Emergency calls

Ambulance (Pronto Soccorso Autoambulanze – Blue Cross)	
Venice	3 00 00
Mestre	98 89 88
Breakdown assistance	116
Emergency (general – fire, ambulance, police)	113
First Aid: (Croce Rossa – Red Cross)	
Venice	8 63 46
Mestre	95 09 88
Ambulatorio Lido	76 87 00
Flying Squad	
Venice	3 60 00
Mestre	5 77 77
Information	
Automobile club Italiano (ACI)	70 03 00
Airlines	
Alitalia	70 03 55
British Airways	8 50 26 (BA)
TWA	70 32 30 (TWA)
Airport	66 12 62
Consulate	
Great Britain	2 72 07
Hospitals	
Ospedale Civile, Venice	70 56 22
Ospedale Civile, Mestre	95 79 44
Ospedale al Mare, Lido	76 01 80
Lost property	
Municipal transport	2 09 21
Police	
Questura (Police Headquarters, Passport and Aliens Department)	70 32 22
Carabinieri, Venice	3 22 22
Carabiniere, Mestre	5 55 55
Polizia Stradala (Traffic police), Mestre	5 61 11, 96 17 22
Vigili Urbani (Municipal police) Venice	2 40 63
Vigili Urbani, Mestre	5 61 03
Tourist offices	
Azienda Autonoma di Soggiorno e Turismo	2 61 10
Uffici Comune Turismo	70 07 92
Uffici Informazioni E.P.T.E.A.A.S.T	2 63 56
Uffici Informazioni F.S. (railways)	51 55 55
Telegrams	8 50 72
Telephone	
Dialling code for the United Kingdom	00 44
Dialling code for Venice from the United Kingdom	010 39 41
Dialling code for Venice from the United States and Canada	011 39 41

Baedeker's Travel Guides

"The maps and illustrations are lavish. The arrangement of information (alphabetically by city) makes it easy to use the book."

—San Francisco Examiner-Chronicle

What's there to do and see in foreign countries? Travelers who rely on Baedeker, one of the oldest names in travel literature, will miss nothing. Baedeker's bright red, internationally recognized covers open up to reveal fascinating A-Z directories of cities, towns, and regions, complete with their sights, museums, monuments, cathedrals, castles, gardens and ancestral homes—an approach that gives the traveler a quick and easy way to plan a vacation itinerary.

And Baedekers are filled with over 200 full-color photos and detailed maps, including a full-size, fold-out roadmap for easy vacation driving. Baedeker—the premier name in travel for over 140 years.

Please send me the books checked below and fill in order form on reverse side.

Please turn the page for an order form and a list of additional Baedeker Guides.

A series of city guides filled with colour photographs and detailed maps and floor plans from one of the oldest names in travel publishing:

Please send me the books checked below:

☐ **Amsterdam** $10.95 0-13-057969-6	☐ **adrid** $10.95 0-13-058033-3
☐ **Athens** $10.95 0-13-057977-7	☐ **Moscow** $10.95 0-13-058041-4
☐ **Bangkok** $10.95 0-13-057985-8	☐ **Munich** $10.95 0-13-370370-3
☐ **Berlin** $10.95 0-13-367996-9	☐ **New York** $10.95 0-13-058058-9
☐ **Brussels** $10.95 0-13-368788-0	☐ **Paris** $10.95 0-13-058066-X
☐ **Copenhagen** $10.95 0-13-057993-9	☐ **Rome** $10.95 0-13-058074-0
☐ **Florence** $10.95 0-13-369505-0	☐ **San Francisco** $10.95 0-13-058082-1
☐ **Frankfurt** $10.95 0-13-369570-0	☐ **Singapore** $10.95 0-13-058090-2
☐ **Hamburg** $10.95 0-13-369687-1	☐ **Tokyo** $10.95 0-13-058108-9
☐ **Hong Kong** $10.95 0-13-058009-0	☐ **Venice** $10.95 0-13-058116-X
☐ **Jerusalem** $10.95 0-13-058017-1	☐ **Vienna** $10.95 0-13-371303-2
☐ **London** $10.95 0-13-058025-2	

PRENTICE HALL PRESS

Order Department—Travel Books

200 Old Tappan Road

Old Tappan, New Jersey 07675

In U.S. include $1 postage and handling for 1st book, 25¢ each additional book. Outside U.S. $2 and 50¢ respectively.

Enclosed is my check or money order for $_____

NAME_____

ADDRESS_____

CITY_____STATE_____ZIP_____